The

ACCIDENTAL

Volunteer Society

A story of tea, chaos, and finding your purpose
completely by mistake

Christopher Hall

Copyright Page

The Accidental Volunteer Society
A story of tea, chaos, and finding your purpose completely by mistake.

For inquiries, permissions, or more information, contact:
chris@christopherjameshall.co.uk

Contents

Welcome to the Beautiful Chaos

There are certain moments in life you don't realise are pivotal until much later.

Like the time you agree to "just one drink" and end up ordering a kebab from a man dressed as a wizard. Or when you Google *ways to feel useful that don't involve spreadsheets* and accidentally sign up to volunteer at a food bank, a drama group, and something mysteriously called *Digital Buddies* - all before your tea's gone cold.

Sam hadn't meant to start anything. She wasn't on a grand quest. She wasn't even dressed properly - wearing one sock, a cardigan that smelt faintly of last night's dinner, and the kind of expression only used for tax returns. The truth was, she just wanted to feel... less useless. More needed. Slightly less like a leftover crumpet in the toaster of life.

So, she volunteered.

Badly.

She got tangled in leads at a dog shelter, outwitted by a pensioner called Trevor, and almost set fire to someone's microwave. At no point did she look like someone who was making a *difference*. But somehow, in the middle of the barking and minor health and safety violations, something began to take shape.

1

It started with friends. Then a group of friends. Then a name they all hated but couldn't think of anything better:

The Workshop Café.

And before she knew it, there were budgeting sessions led by people who once hid from bank statements, kids learning drama from a woman with more scarves than sense, and Mo - lovely, quiet Mo - sewing dignity into torn hoodies and people's hearts alike.

Some days it was students practising English, other days it was pensioners just grateful for a chair that wasn't their own kitchen table.

It wasn't professional. It wasn't planned. And it definitely wasn't funded.

But it worked.

Because sometimes, showing up - awkwardly, accidentally, arms full of biscuits and self-doubt - is all it takes.

This is not a guidebook. It won't teach you how to volunteer properly, or run a community project, or avoid supergluing your sleeve to a chair (though that last one is mostly about staying calm and owning fewer cardigans).

What it will do is introduce you to a group of people who didn't set out to start anything either.

They just cared.

They didn't always know what they were doing, but they showed up. With snacks. With stories. With skills they didn't know they had.

This is a story about that. About kindness without strategy. About community built out of burnt pies and power poses and coat racks where no one's coat ever gets judged.

It's about what can happen when you stop waiting to be useful and start being honest instead.

And yes - it's about biscuits.

Always biscuits.

Welcome to The Workshop Café.

We're glad you're here.

Trial by Tea Break

The Biscuit Crisis

Sam glared at her laptop screen like it had just stolen her last biscuit. Which, in fairness, it might as well have.

'Data Reconciliation Assistant,' it read.

She wrinkled her nose. *Data Reconciliation Assistant* sounded like the kind of job where your biggest thrill was colour-coding spreadsheets and apologising to printers. Possibly while becoming one with a swivel chair.

She muttered, "If I'm your idea of a data reconciliation assistant, you probably need to reconcile your expectations," and clicked away before her brain turned to mush.

There it was again. The same sinking feeling. Not quite failure, not quite panic - more like the sensation you get when someone says, *"Tell us a fun fact about yourself!"* at a networking event.

Sam slouched back in her chair - one of Ronnie's rejects from the café, now doing a second career in her kitchen - and dunked a custard cream. It crumbled mid-dunk, gave up on life, and disappeared into her tea like it knew exactly what kind of morning it was.

She fished it out with a spoon, stared at its soggy remains, and sighed. "Same, mate."

Six months out of Uni, and this was it. Biscuits and tea. Disappointment. And the slow, creeping suspicion that everyone else was out there thriving while she was stuck in limbo with a dying plant and 94 unread job alerts.

She used to be in everything - student radio, the theatre group, some slightly culty climate society where people made banners out of old bedsheets and emotional trauma. It all felt important then. Like she was on the verge of becoming something.

Now? Now she worked part-time in a tea shop with a terrifyingly low ceiling and a boss who used sarcasm like most people used breathing.

She clicked open another job ad.

Graduate opportunity:

Corporate Systems Integration Officer.

"Stop trying to make 'graduate opportunity' sound exciting," she muttered. "We both know it's code for human printer support."

Her laptop pinged. New suggestion:

Risk Management Coordinator.

She stared at it. "No. Absolutely not. I can barely coordinate socks."

Sam closed the laptop with the solemn authority of someone ending a bad date and stared into space. The kitchen was silent except for the distant hum of the fridge and the quiet rustle of Barry the plant leaning aggressively towards the light like he had big photosynthesis plans.

She stood up, walked to the kettle, and declared, "I need to do something useful."

The kettle, to its credit, started boiling without judgement.

Tea in hand, she pulled out her phone and typed, "ways to feel useful that don't involve Lycra or pyramid schemes".

Autocorrect changed it to *Lycra or parrots*.

Honestly? Still accurate.

She scrolled. Clicked. And there it was - a volunteering website.

Make a difference in your community!

No experience necessary!

Perfect. She had *loads* of no experience.

She sipped, scrolled, clicked:

- One for a charity shop
- One for dog-walking
- One for befriending an older person

Each click felt strangely powerful. Like she was doing something. Moving. Even if it was just moving in the vague direction of 'Doing a Thing.'

Then she paused.

"What if they actually... reply?"

Too late. Her inbox pinged.

Subject:

Volunteer Opportunity Confirmation – Welcome!

Oh no.

She was in.

Trial shift. Charity shop. Tomorrow. 10am.

'Arrive in comfortable shoes with a friendly attitude.'

Sam looked down at her slippers. "Comfortable, yes. Friendly? Not unless you count being held together by glue and desperation."

She opened the group chat.

Sam: I may have just accidentally signed up to save the world. Or fold donated jeans. Unsure. Either way... help.

Tasha: "You volunteering?? I need to see a video."

Rupa: "Proud of you! I'm only helping if I don't have to wear a lanyard."

Mo: Just sent a thumbs up emoji.

Lee: No response. Probably still thinks WhatsApp is a type of sandwich.

Sam smiled. Her friends were chaos in human form, but they got her. They'd been through bad performances, long nights, cold protests, and one unforgettable incident involving a jelly mould and a squirrel.

This couldn't be worse than that. Surely.

She drained her tea, gave Barry a reassuring nod ("You'll cope without me for a day"), and started planning. Sort of. Mostly staring at the wardrobe and wondering which outfit said, *I'm friendly, but please don't leave me alone at the till.*

Her phone buzzed again.

Tasha: "I'll come by with coffee before your shift. Civic engagement needs caffeine."

Rupa: "Also bring snacks. And spare socks. In that order."

Mo: Liked the message. Again. Probably lying under a blanket in solidarity.

Sam exhaled, full of nervous energy and wondering why she needed spare socks. She didn't know if this would be it - the thing that made her feel like herself again - but at least she wasn't just scrolling job ads and yelling at the kettle anymore.

She was doing something.

Something small.

Something un-beige.

And that felt like a start.

As she cleaned the mug, recycled the biscuit wrapper (probably incorrectly), and tried not to trip over the same slipper again, she muttered, "You've got this."

The microwave glinted back at her with the quiet disbelief of an appliance that had seen too much.

Still, she grinned.

She was going out tomorrow.

To volunteer.

To wear real trousers.

To be... useful.

Probably.

But first, another tea.

Charity Shop Shenanigans

Sam arrived five minutes early, mostly because she wanted to make a good impression - and partially because she hadn't trusted Google Maps and had left the house like she was embarking on a pilgrimage. After years of coexisting with her sofa, a walk to the high street felt like an expedition. She even packed a cereal bar. Just in case.

The charity shop looked smaller in person. Cosy, cluttered, and filled with the very specific scent that can only be described as *Eau de Second-Hand*. It was part lavender, part church hall, with subtle notes of warm fabric softener and ancient book spine. A sort of vintage potpourri meets nostalgia and mothballs.

The sign in the window read:

SALE

All scarves £1, unless highly significant.

Sam wasn't sure if that was a joke or just brutally honest stock control.

She stepped inside. A woman in her late sixties looked up from steaming a floral blouse with the kind of laser focus typically seen in international espionage. Her badge read *Delia*, but her expression read *Don't test me*.

"You must be the volunteer," Delia said, without a hint of question or welcome.

Sam nodded, trying to exude 'cheerful helper' while discreetly wiping a suspicious biscuit flake from her sleeve. "I'm Sam. First day. Well... only day. Maybe. We'll see how much property damage I cause."

Delia squinted, like she'd just been offered a tofu bacon sandwich.

"We're short on hangers, patience, and people who can tell beige from greige," she said briskly. "You'll be sorting donations. Try not to break the label gun. Again."

Sam blinked. "Sorry - *again*?"

"Pre-emptive warning."

Right. Okay then.

Sam tried to smile in a way that *said I am very capable and unlikely to cause havoc*, while internally screaming "*WHAT IS GREIGE?!*"

Delia pointed towards the back room, where a small mountain of donations loomed like the forgotten offspring of a laundry basket and a time machine.

And so, the shift began.

Task One: The Avalanche of Unwashed Potential

The donation pile was not so much a pile as it was a small Alp of textiles - a Mount Jumpers, if you will. It spilled from the donation bin like it had been waiting centuries to breathe again.

The donation mountain revealed treasures beyond imagination: jumpers that smelled of cat, dog, and every animal in between; trousers with more buttons than sense; three mismatched wellies (none forming a pair); and a mug shaped like a dolphin mid-backflip.

Sam attempted organization with a color-coded rail system - an unsolicited effort she hoped might earn Delia's approval. Spoiler: it didn't.

When she discovered a vintage jacket reminiscent of *Murder, She Wrote* fashion, she priced it at £4.50 using her sophisticated valuation method: "looks nice + feels luxurious."

The next hour featured:

- Hair tangled in a rotating clothes rail
- One toppled mannequin leg (just the limb)
- 47 apologies (12 directed at inanimate objects)

Delia observed with the quiet intensity of a former headmistress who could still wither souls with a single arched brow. Her muttered "This isn't the V&A" left Sam wondering if it was critique or life advice.

Then came The Loo Incident.

It began simply, a sprightly customer (the lemon-drizzle-baking type) requested restroom directions. Sam helpfully indicated the backroom door that absolutely appeared to be a toilet.

It was technically a toilet.

The lock, however, had retired circa 1992, a casualty of 'budgetary mystery.'

Ten minutes later, "Excuse me? Hello? I think I'm... um... trapped?"

Sam froze. Delia materialized like a spectre summoned by mild inconvenience. "Well," she declared, arms folded. "That's a first."

Sam's "I'll fix it!" came out several octaves higher than intended.

The rescue operation required:

- One reformed coat hanger
- Three apologetic door-conversations
- A baffling hinge discussion neither participant understood

The liberated customer emerged flushed but cheerful, clutching a '*Hot Stuff*' mug and declaring, "Well, that's my cardio for the week!"

Sam, vibrating with guilt, offered the customer a scarf as compensation. Delia intercepted it mid-air. "We're not running a charity here."

New volunteer lesson learned:

Customer imprisonment = generally frowned upon.

By lunch, Sam resembled a frazzled science experiment - drained and crackling with static from the polyester donation bin. She stole a glance at her phone beneath the counter while Delia attacked what might have once been a skirt with the steamer.

Rupa: "How's the first shift?"

Sam: "I may have broken fashion. And possibly someone's bladder."

Mo: "Metaphor?"

Sam: "No."

Mo: "Oh."

The afternoon passed with fewer catastrophes, though Sam did have an unexpectedly profound therapy session with a one-eyed teddy bear. It was surprisingly good at listening.

As closing time approached, Sam hovered by the exit - uncertain whether to formally clock out or simply disappear. Delia arrived out of nowhere with a paper rota.

"Tuesdays work for you?"

"I'm... not certain yet," Sam hedged, aiming for neutral politeness that screamed *please never trust me with toilet-related responsibilities again*.

Delia's penetrating stare could have sterilized surgical equipment. Then - so fleeting Sam almost missed it - the corner of her mouth twitched. Not quite a smile. More like a facial muscle spasm with potential.

"You're chaotic," Delia declared. "But you care. We get worse."

Sam wasn't entirely sure she'd been complimented, but it was absolutely going in her CV's 'skills' section.

Stepping outside, Sam blinked in the daylight. Against all odds, she'd survived. She'd labelled. She'd folded. She'd briefly turned a pensioner into an unwilling escape room participant, but she'd survived.

That evening, over Rupa's 'rustic' lasagne (translation: charcoal-adjacent but made with affection), the full story emerged.

"You locked someone in the toilet?" Tasha laughed, tears streaming.

"Temporarily! She had beverages! She was fine!"

Lee nodded solemnly. "This will be her legacy. 'Survived the Blitz and one shift with Sam.'"

Sam face-planted into garlic bread. "At least I priced the clothes correctly."

Rupa cleared her throat. "About that Harris Tweed in the window..."

Sam's head snapped up. "How do you know it's Harris Tweed?"

"I did a welfare check around lunch. You looked... disturbingly happy pricing jumpers, so I left you to it." Rupa paused. "That jacket's vintage 1970s. Worth about £300. What number did you write on the tag?"

Sam froze.

"Oh."

Mo gently handed her a biscuit. "You tried. That's what matters."

"I almost sold a vintage heirloom for the price of a flat white."

"Still counts," said Tasha.

Ronnie, who'd been quietly refilling the sugar jar, muttered without looking up, "If you bring glitter into that shop, you will be disowned."

Sam leaned back, lasagne in her belly and laughter in her lungs. She'd done a thing. An actual thing. And she hadn't imploded.

Tomorrow was dog-walking.

What could possibly go wrong?

Paw Patrol Panic

Sam had pictured something serene.

You know the kind - a light breeze, a leafy park, birds tweeting (but not in the aggressive, bin-divey way), and a small, grateful rescue dog trotting alongside her, gazing up like she'd just reinvented chicken. She imagined this hypothetical dog would be called something adorable, like Biscuit or Waffles, and they'd bond over a shared dislike of joggers and cold weather.

Instead, she got Nigel.

Nigel was a chihuahua.

But not the handbag kind. Oh no.

Nigel was a five-kilogram warlord with the bark of a malfunctioning smoke alarm and the eyes of someone who's seen things. Terrible things. He greeted Sam by launching himself at her shoe with the velocity of a rogue tennis ball and the rage of a caffeinated toddler who's just been told nap time is non-negotiable.

"That's Nigel," said the rescue centre manager, with the tone of someone who had fully accepted her fate. She handed Sam a bundle of leads that resembled a spaghetti-based horror story. "He's got... trust issues. And enthusiasm."

Sam nodded like she understood. She did not. At all. But she smiled anyway, because that's what polite people do when handed a problem disguised as a dog.

She crouched down and said, with the same energy one might reserve for a sacred monk, "Hi, Nigel!"

Nigel growled, locked eyes with her... and promptly peed on her sock.

Stunning start.

She was technically meant to walk four dogs. Four. At once. Like some sort of benevolent octopus on a quest for enlightenment.

Alongside Nigel (tiny, demonic), there was:

- Pickle – a greyhound with the permanent expression of someone who's just been surprised by a loud sneeze.
- Brenda – a lab mix roughly the size of a sofa and built like she'd been raised on protein shakes and tractor-pulling contests.
- Elton – a shih tzu who walked like he was late for a red carpet and had absolutely no time for nonsense.

It was supposed to be a "gentle enrichment walk."

Instead, it became a tactical survival exercise.

By minute five, Sam had been:

- Headbutted by Nigel (intentionally, she swore),

- Put to the test by Pickle, who kept tripping over his own legs like he was unfamiliar with gravity.
- Dragged sideways by Brenda chasing a leaf, and
- Spun in three circles by Elton's dramatic zigzagging.

"Who's walking who?!" called a woman from across the park, laughing.

"Honestly?" Sam yelled back. "No one. It's a democracy now. Possibly a coup."

Nigel then lunged at a butterfly with the same commitment most people reserve for Black Friday TVs and nearly dislocated her elbow.

There was a moment - somewhere between Brenda trying to eat a pinecone and Elton attempting to flirt with a garden gnome - when Sam genuinely considered just sitting on the pavement and waiting for the chaos to pass. Like a very tired traffic cone.

Eventually, they reached a patch of grass that appeared to contain *neither* wildlife *nor* joggers. Sam exhaled, like someone who'd just survived an unexpected hurricane made of teeth and fur.

She perched on a bench, covered in mud, hair static, and a vague dampness she didn't care to investigate.

Nigel glared at her from beneath the bench like she owed him money.

Elton struck a pose on top like he was waiting for his Vogue shoot.

Brenda rolled in something unspeakable.

Pickle sat down and looked like he needed therapy.

Sam reached for her phone. This was going to be funny later. It had to be. Please let it be.

Mo: "How's the walk?"

Sam: "I have seen things."

Mo: "That good?"

Sam: "I think Nigel might be the devil."

That afternoon, Sam arrived at Ronnie's Café looking like she'd lost a fight with a sentient hoover bag.

Rupa, who was seated at their usual table with the rest of her friends, took one look and gestured her over like a seasoned medic. "Oh, love. Sit down. I've ordered tea and I have a lint roller in my bag."

Over a moment of empathy and shared trauma, Sam told the tale.

The sock wee. The butterfly ambush. The spontaneous interpretive dance Brenda performed on the bandstand. Nigel's vendetta against pigeons, joggers, and specifically anyone wearing beige.

Tasha clapped at the end like it was performance art. "Honestly, I'd pay to see that."

"I nearly did a full forward roll trying to retrieve a poo bag," said Sam, staring into her tea.

"Even better!" Tasha beamed. "Poo-bag parkour!"

Mo, who had arrived mid-story and had been quietly sipping his tea like an emotional support brew, finally asked, "Were they... cute, though?"

Sam didn't break eye contact. "Mo. I Googled 'Can chihuahuas be evil?' in the car park."

Lee, silent as ever, had to hide his face behind a cushion to muffle the sound of his laughter.

"I think I need a new hobby," Sam sighed, flopping backwards dramatically.

"You just need something better to care for," said Rupa, poking her with a fork. "Like a houseplant. Or one of those rocks people used to talk to in the '90s."

"I have Barry."

"Barry doesn't try to eat your ankles."

"No, but he leans at me when I forget to water him. With intent."

There was a pause. Tasha's brain, as ever, was clearly revving up to something.

"We should make a group," she said.

"A support group for traumatised dog walkers?" Sam asked.

"No! I mean... yes, but no. Like, a thing. Where we try new stuff. Share skills. Help each other out. Not just dodge Nigel and lose the will to live."

Mo raised an eyebrow. "I don't have any skills."

"You built a wardrobe for your niece last Christmas."

"I followed instructions."

"It was IKEA."

"I followed difficult instructions."

Sam sat up. "So, like a weird club? For people who don't quite know what they're doing but want to feel... less useless?"

Tasha nodded enthusiastically. "Exactly! No pressure. No 'you must be brilliant'. Just... show up. Try something. Drink tea. Don't get wee'd on."

From the kitchen, a voice muttered, "Sounds like chaos with admin."

It was Ronnie. They emerged with a tray of teacups and the expression of someone permanently halfway between "I love you lot" and "Why do I let you in my café."

Sam grinned. "My favourite kind of chaos."

Ronnie rolled their eyes. "Fine. But if anyone brings glitter, I'm locking the door."

And that, as it turns out, was the beginning of something.

They didn't know it yet. But between Brenda's breakdancing, Nigel's fury, and Sam's dramatic dog-lead tango, something had shifted.

They'd walked dogs, yes. Badly. But they'd also walked themselves somewhere new. Somewhere messier, stranger, and unexpectedly lovely.

The Workshop Café hadn't been born yet.

But the idea had just peed on its first sock.

.

Tea with Trevor

The instructions had been very clear.

"Just pop in for a friendly chat. He's lovely. Bit eccentric. Likes tea."

Which, in volunteer-speak, could mean anything from "he owns a cat that bites" to "prepare for an accidental séance."

Sam stood outside the small bungalow with the kind of cautious optimism often applied to suspicious contents in Tupperware and blind dates with someone who "looks nothing like their profile, but in a good way."

She had already delivered herself a motivational speech in the car.

"Be warm. Be open. Do not spill anything. Again."

She adjusted her jacket, took a breath, and rang the bell.

The door creaked open like something from a 1970s horror movie.

Trevor appeared, tall and wiry, with hair like startled thistledown and a cardigan that had more pockets than a magician's top hat. Possibly because it was a magician's top hat. Around his neck was a cravat that had clearly lived through several significant historical events.

"You must be the volunteer," he said, peering at her like she might be an apparition.

"That's me. Sam."

"Are you real?"

She blinked. "I think so?"

He gave a theatrical nod. "Hmm. That's what the last one said."

Then, with a grand sweep of his arm.

"Enter, if you dare!"

She dared. She entered.

Trevor's living room was a fever dream of time, clutter, and showmanship. It looked like an antique shop and a circus tent had eloped, moved in together, and never cleaned out the attic.

Stacks of newspapers. Shelves of books with titles like *The Mildly Useful Guide to Card Tricks* and *The Conspiracy Theorist's Almanac: Volume II*. A stuffed owl wearing a fez glared at her from the mantelpiece. A top hat sat on a floral armchair like it had squatter's rights.

A radio in the corner played swing jazz, just loud enough to suggest it had opinions.

Trevor gestured to the sofa like he was about to host *Countdown*.

"Tea?"

"Yes please."

"Brandy?"

"Oh. Um - "

"It's medicinal," he said, pouring a generous splash into two wildly mismatched mugs before she could finish hesitating.

The tea tasted like a hot, floral slap to the senses. Sam sipped and smiled through the internal combustion.

Trevor settled into his squeaky throne of an armchair and looked at her like she'd just pulled a rabbit out of a hat.

"So, why'd they send you?"

"I signed up to befriend someone," she said, carefully not tipping her brandy-tea onto her lap. "Just here for a chat, really."

"A chat! Splendid. Shall I go first?"

She nodded. Resistance was futile.

"I was a magician," he declared. "Not professionally. But I once made a sausage roll disappear from three feet away."

She raised an eyebrow.

"It was in someone else's lunchbox. Bit of a misunderstanding."

He reached into his cardigan - from somewhere near pocket six or seven - and produced a playing card. He held it out like he was revealing prophecy.

"Your destiny," he said gravely.

She turned it over. Queen of Hearts. Of course.

Trevor talked. A lot. But not in a way that made you want to leave. More like someone unspooling a box of dusty treasures.

He told her about working in insurance ("It was 90% hole punching, 10% mild panic"), his late wife Audrey ("A stunning woman. Strong opinions. Terrible at Scrabble. Wouldn't let me use 'abracadabra'"), and his absolute certainty that pigeons were not birds, but highly trained spies in feathery disguises.

Sam laughed more in that one hour than she had all week.

In return, she shared some of her volunteering misadventures.

Trevor wheezed with delight, slapped his knee, and offered her a biscuit that disintegrated on contact like a biscuit-shaped sigh.

"You're a good sort," he said.

Sam wasn't sure what sort that was, but it felt like a compliment carved out of oddness and affection.

The only moment of panic came when she gently asked how he was keeping, and he responded by closing his eyes and slumping dramatically.

She gasped.

Three seconds of internal screaming later, he peeked open one eye and whispered, "Kidding. I just enjoy the drama."

She almost hit him with the brandy-tea. Almost.

When it was time to leave, she stood reluctantly.

"Already?"

"They said to keep it short for the first visit."

"Cowards," he muttered.

She picked up her coat, now subtly infused with the scents of Earl Grey and eccentricity.

"Thank you for the tea. And the... card trick."

Trevor stood and gave a small theatrical bow. "Come back next week. I'll teach you how to make a teaspoon vanish."

"I'd love that."

He leaned in. "Don't tell the pigeons."

She stepped out into the cold afternoon and felt warmer than she had in days.

Later, back at the café, she recounted the whole story with the air of someone who'd just returned from Narnia.

"A magician?" Rupa said, eyes wide. "You got the best one!"

"He put brandy in the tea," Sam replied.

"Even better!"

"Are we not going to talk about the pigeons?" asked Mo, raising an eyebrow.

"He genuinely believes they're spies for the Government."

Mo nodded solemnly. "Honestly? Checks out."

Ronnie passed with a tray of coffees and muttered, "As long as he doesn't show up here in a cape, I'll allow it."

"He might," Sam said with a grin. "And if he does, I'm saving him a seat."

Because for the first time in a long time, Sam had felt... seen.

Not for her usefulness, or her attempt at doing things "right," but just for turning up.

No glitter. No expectations. Just tea, talk, and a pocket full of card tricks.

And maybe, just maybe, that was enough.

Until next time, Trevor.

And pigeons - you've been warned.

A Short-Lived Shift

Sam arrived at the church hall ten minutes early, not because she was organised, but because she'd overestimated the bus schedule, arrived forty minutes early and had been loitering outside like someone auditioning for a very low-budget heist film. She had a notepad in one hand, nerves in the other, and wore a T-shirt that declared in big, bold pink letters:

'HERE TO HELP'.

It was a gift from Rupa. Rupa had also offered to iron it. Rupa had promptly forgotten and handed it over with a shrug and a faint smell of lasagne.

The church hall smelled like most church halls: instant coffee, damp hymnals, and mild despair. Rows of folding tables stretched across the room like the low-budget cousin of Supermarket Sweep, and boxes of donations teetered like a game of Jenga being played by toddlers on a sugar high.

A sign above the kettle read:

DON'T TOUCH THIS. IT LEAKS.

Someone had also added:

(AND SO DOES MARGARET.)

Sam didn't know who Margaret was, but she immediately wanted to befriend her.

"Ah! You must be the new volunteer!" A cheerfully frazzled woman with an ambitious fringe and the energy of someone who ran on leftover biscuits waved her in. "I'm Pauline. You can start by sorting those tins."

Sam nodded enthusiastically. Tins. She could do tins. This was it. Her redemption arc. Her cinematic training montage, just with more baked beans.

She approached the table like a contestant on The Great British Sort-Off. The tins were in semi-disorganised chaos. Condensed milk was mingling with custard. Beans were having a party with spaghetti hoops. One tin just said 'Meat' with a slightly threatening wobble, like it knew secrets.

"I'll just... organise these," she said with all the confidence of someone who once arranged her kitchen drawers by material — wood with wood, steel with steel, plastic with plastic, as if she were curating a museum of spoons."

"Brilliant," said Pauline. "Chuck anything with a dent you can fit a pencil in. And remember - custard's a dessert, not a staple."

Sam nodded.

And at once forgot everything Pauline had just said.

She decided on a system. Alphabetical. Logical. Beautiful. This would be her masterpiece. This would be art.

Potatoes, stewed steak, sweetcorn. Everything had its place. Her towers rose like monuments to canned efficiency. Margaret (of the mysterious leakage) shuffled past and offered her a bourbon cream, like a tiny, biscuit-based knighthood. Sam beamed.

Things were going well.

And then came... *The Custard Incident.*

"Excuse me?" said a voice behind her.

Sam turned to find a man in a hi-vis vest holding two children and a shopping list. He looked like a man on a mission. A custard-based mission.

He pointed at the custard tower. "Are these not included?"

"Oh, they're in the dessert section," Sam replied brightly. "This table is all the cupboard essentials."

The man blinked.

"Custard is essential," he said, very seriously. "You ever tried feeding a toddler plain rice pudding?"

One of the children gave a solemn nod. "It's sad."

Sam faltered. "Right. Of course. I didn't mean to say it wasn't essential, I just... filed it under 'treats'?"

A queue had formed behind them. Someone wanted gravy granules. Someone else was searching for pineapple chunks. A third person was holding up a can of creamed mushrooms like it was a crime scene exhibit.

Pauline returned just in time to find Sam in the eye of a very polite, tinned-goods-related storm.

"What on earth is going on?" she asked, surveying what was now less of a system and more of a philosophical debate.

Sam looked up, hair slightly static from all the plastic wrap, and said, "I think I started a movement. The custard people are organising."

Pauline raised an eyebrow.

"They're passionate," Sam added, gesturing to the queue. "One of them quoted Delia Smith. About moral priorities."

Pauline sighed, long and deep. "Just... go help with packing. We'll sort the tins later."

Sam nodded and retreated like a confused librarian at a rock concert.

Behind her, a woman loudly declared, "I don't care what the sign says. Custard goes with everything."

In the packing section, Sam did her best to redeem herself. All she had to do was put items in bags. Easy. No politics. No custard.

Except she got stuck on pasta. Fusilli or penne?

Penne felt aggressive.

Fusilli felt indecisive.

She dithered.

Then she packed a parcel with toilet paper and baked beans in the same bag. Twice.

She dropped a jar of peanut butter on her own foot. Apologised to it. Then apologised again to the shelf.

By the end of the shift, she'd muttered "sorry" at least seventeen times - to humans, tins, and one mildly judgmental bottle of own-brand ketchup.

Pauline, to her credit, handed her a biscuit on the way out.

"You're enthusiastic," she said kindly.

Sam nodded, brushing bean dust from her sleeve. "And mildly incompetent."

Pauline smiled. "That's most of us, love."

Later, back at the café, Sam collapsed into a chair like she had just completed the London Marathon dressed as a novelty chicken.

"I may have caused a civil war," she announced. "About custard."

Ronnie appeared with a tray of tea and the look of someone who'd seen worse. Possibly in the alley behind the bins.

"Volunteering?"

Sam nodded.

"Food bank?"

Another nod.

Ronnie poured the tea. "Sounds about right."

Rupa arrived just in time to hear the phrase *'nostalgic categories of tinned goods'* and immediately lost it, wheezing into her scarf.

"Please tell me everything."

Sam did.

The alphabetised tins.

The uprising.

The Delia Smith quote.

The fusilli-panic and the bean-and-bog-roll combo.

Tasha grabbed a napkin and started sketching. "I'm making a 'Custard is Essential' campaign poster."

Mo, ever practical, offered to create a spreadsheet. "We could colour-code by mood. Yellow for cheer. Brown for existential dread. Pink for nostalgia."

"I'm not sure they'll let me back," Sam muttered.

"They will," said Rupa. "They always need people."

"Even chaotic ones?"

"Especially chaotic ones."

Sam sipped her tea and stared into the middle distance.

She'd tried.

She'd possibly restructured the entire concept of food categories.

She may have emotionally scarred a tin of marrowfat peas.

But she'd shown up.

Somewhere, out there, a child was eating custard.

Not as a treat.

Not as a luxury.

But as an essential part of their dinner.

And smiling.

She raised her mug.

To custard.

To kindness.

And to very, very patient food bank managers.

Drama Club Debacle

Sam had agreed to help with the local youth drama group because the words *"It'll be fun!"* had been said. Twice. Possibly three times. Definitely with jazz hands.

"Just light support," the organiser had promised. "Handing out juice, maybe helping with props."

Sam could handle juice. She had a degree in juice distribution, unofficially earned at every children's party she'd ever survived. Props? Fine. Props were inanimate and rarely asked questions.

What she was not prepared for, however, was becoming a tree.

The drama group met in the community centre - a building that smelt permanently of orange squash and misplaced coats. The kind of place where dreams were born, crushed, revived with biscuits, and then turned into papier-mâché monsters.

The walls were plastered with rainbows, motivational slogans, and something in the corner that might once have been a camel but now resembled a melted handbag on stilts.

Naturally, it was Tasha who'd volunteered Sam for the role.

"You'll be brilliant," she'd said, with the same confidence one might use to convince someone to jump off a pier. "It's all about confidence!"

Sam, whose last theatrical experience involved hiding behind a curtain during *Bugsy Malone,* had nodded with the haunted expression of someone who'd just agreed to babysit a badger.

Upon arrival, she was introduced to a blur of children ranging in age from seven to "legal chaos."

One small boy shouted, "I smell biscuits!" and attempted to open her backpack like a raccoon in a heist movie.

Another just handed her a plastic sword and walked away without explanation.

They began with "warm-ups," which Sam assumed meant light stretching and maybe a quick chat about the play.

It did not.

It meant pretending to be uncooked spaghetti, melting into puddles, rebirthing into sunflowers, and navigating a room full of sticky-fingered human hurricanes.

All before she'd had tea.

The children, however, were wonderful. Loud, messy, and fully committed.

One small boy declared himself "here for the sword fights."

A girl in a unicorn t-shirt narrated her entire existence in third person.

"And now I'm walking. And now I'm turning. And now I'm judging you."

Sam liked her immediately.

Halfway through the session, Tasha swept in wearing a scarf that could double as a glider and a face full of purpose.

"Darlings!" she called, flinging her arms wide. "Let's rehearse the forest scene! We start with the woodland! Sam - you're a tree!"

Sam blinked. "Sorry - what?"

"You're the tree," Tasha repeated, as if it were the most natural progression in the world.

"I thought I was doing juice?"

"Trees don't talk," the unicorn girl informed her solemnly.

Tasha clapped her hands. "Come on! Stillness! Strength! Woodland energy!"

Sam, whose idea of woodland energy mostly involved hiding from midges and Googling "how poisonous is nettle rash," reluctantly shuffled to the back of the room and assumed what she hoped was a convincingly arboreal pose.

Turns out, *being a tree is incredibly difficult.*

First, she had to stand completely still. Already a challenge for someone whose internal anxiety made her vibrate slightly at all times. Then she had to *look tree-like*.

What did that mean? Arms up? Out? One bent elbow like a branch? What kind of tree was she, anyway? Beech? Oak? Emotionally withered bonsai?

A child poked her shin. "Are you oak?"

"I'm... trying," she whispered.

The scene began.

A boy leapt forward with the confidence of someone raised on action movies.

"I am Sir Galloping Hamstring, and I will defeat the darkness!" he bellowed, brandishing his plastic sword like a baguette of justice.

Another child declared herself "Queen of the Caterpillars" and proceeded to writhe across the floor in what Sam could only describe as interpretive soil surfing.

Sam did her best. She stood tall. Rooted. Verdant. The very essence of silent, stoic foliage.

For thirty seconds.

Then someone sneezed nearby. Loudly.

She flinched.

Her branch-arms wobbled. Her knees bent.

And in what could only be described as a very slow tree-based trust fall, she toppled backwards into a cardboard scenery pile.

Specifically, into the papier-mâché rock - which, it turned out, hadn't been fully dry since the 2016 Summer Pantomime.

It collapsed on impact like a wet sponge.

Children shrieked with joy.

Tasha clapped enthusiastically.

"Brilliant commitment! So real! So grounded in the moment!"

Sam lay in a pile of fake moss.

Once the session ended and the kids had been collected, some still trembling with excitement – or it could have been sugar, Tasha turned to Sam with the grin of someone who had just *delighted* in a natural disaster.

"You were wonderful," she said.

"I was scenery."

"Yes, but scenery with gravitas. You fell with passion. The boulder believed in you."

"One of them called me Miss Wobble Tree."

"That's basically a superhero name."

They made their way back to the café, Sam still carrying a sense of confusion.

The rest of the gang was already there, mid-debrief.

Rupa looked up. "How was the drama group?"

"I achieved full foliage," Sam muttered.

"She was *brilliant*," Tasha declared. "It was like waiting, like the trees dropping their leaves."

Sam groaned. "I fell backwards into a papier-mâché rock and crushed a five-year-old's caterpillar throne."

Rupa winced. "Is she okay?"

"She applauded. Apparently, it added narrative tension."

Ronnie, as ever, arrived with tea at just the right moment and slid a mug across the table.

"You keep this up and I'm going to start charging you rent for your crises."

Sam took the tea with reverence. "That's fair."

Mo looked up from his crossword. "Let's recap. So far, you've volunteered in a charity shop, walked rabid dogs, triggered a custard-based uprising, and now you've performed as a tree."

Sam sighed. "When you put it like that, it sounds like I'm collecting plot points for a surreal humorous fiction novel."

Tasha beamed. "It's a journey."

Lee, quietly fixing the wonky sugar jar, muttered, "All experience is useful, eventually."

Sam leaned back, sticky with glue residue, vaguely damp from the boulder collapse, and unsure whether she could ever look at papier-mâché without a slight twitch.

But there was something stirring.

If this was volunteering - chaotic, unpredictable, bizarrely heartwarming - maybe she had accidentally found something she didn't know she needed. A reason to get involved. To laugh. To be ridiculous. To try.

Even if she wasn't good at it.

Even if she occasionally demolished caterpillar royalty.

She was showing up.

Sam's Weekly Debrief

Every Saturday at exactly 11:03 - not 11:00, because that would imply structure - Sam and her assorted band of life's outtakes gathered at Perk Up Café for what they affectionately called *Mutually Assured Distraction*.

There was no agenda. No goals. No leadership. Just tea, toast, and the shared, unspoken understanding that life was confusing, people were weird, and custard was absolutely not up for debate.

Sam arrived with her usual tote bag, which today contained one packet of biscuits, one folded-up flyer for "Opportunities in Community Litter Action," and approximately seven kilos of baggage. She dropped the lot into the corner booth like a vintage movie heroine collapsing onto a couch.

Ronnie, the café owner, raised a single unimpressed eyebrow and handed her a mug already halfway full. Ronnie never poured tea so much as judged it into existence.

"You look like someone who tried to save the world and failed."

Sam took the mug and sighed. "I may have accidentally reclassified custard as a luxury item and triggered a small revolution."

Ronnie nodded. "Monster."

Moments later, the booth filled like a sitcom opening sequence.

Rupa arrived next, bursting in with Tupperware and big maternal energy. "I made banana bread! With love. And also desperation. It was going off, and I panicked."

She slid the tin across. "Mum always says wasting food is basically a crime. She once made me rescue a pan of lentils with nothing but a spoon."

Mo slid in behind her, wordless as ever, and immediately produced a spare phone charger from his pocket like a socially anxious magician. He plugged it in and sat down, already halfway into a sudoku he wasn't even looking at.

Tasha swept through the door wearing a scarf that had its own gravitational pull. "I just came from toddler ballet. Got kicked during 'Twinkle, Twinkle.' It hurt."

Lee arrived last, as always, quietly placing a small toolbox on the table and fixing the wobbly chair without being asked. He said nothing. He didn't have to. His face said, *I am here. I am mildly tired. I will silently repair this broken world, one misaligned screw at a time.*

Sam sipped her tea. "So, volunteering update. As you know, I've done four things this week, and I think only one of them counts as a success."

"Which one?" asked Rupa, passing around banana bread like communion.

"Tea with Trevor."

"The magician?"

"He put brandy in my tea and explained how pigeons are actually drones working for the government."

Mo raised an eyebrow. "Sounds legit."

"I'm going back next week."

"What about the others?" asked Tasha, flipping open her ever-present rehearsal pad, as if anything Sam said might be relevant for her next fringe play.

Sam groaned. "Charity shop shift ended with someone locked in the loo. Food bank became a battleground over the classification of custard. Dog-walking nearly dislocated my elbow thanks to a chihuahua named Nigel. And I got cast as a tree in the children's drama group."

There was a long, reverent pause.

"You... dressed as a tree?" Rupa managed carefully.

Sam nodded. "I was atmosphere. Still. Leaf-adjacent."

"Did you mean to be a tree?" Mo asked.

"No. The role was thrust upon me. It was that or be the caterpillar queen."

"You came home covered in leaves," said Rupa. "I thought you'd joined a cult."

"I might have. There was chanting. And papier-mâché."

Lee, mid-chew, finally looked up. "You've had quite the week."

"I feel like an enthusiastic tornado with access to a volunteer database."

Tasha grinned and patted her arm. "You were an amazing tree. And it's still better than being a couch potato."

Mo nodded sagely. "You're out there. You're doing stuff."

"Badly," Sam pointed out.

"For real," corrected Tasha.

Ronnie loomed behind them with a teapot and the face of someone who's seen every kind of human nonsense and will still put the kettle on for it.

"You lot always this dramatic?"

"No," Sam said. "Sometimes we're worse."

Ronnie refilled everyone's mugs with a theatrical sigh only achieved by those who've seen true glitter-based trauma.

"If I let you stay here any longer, you'll form some kind of committee."

Tasha's eyes sparkled. "We could!"

"No glitter," Ronnie said immediately.

"I didn't say glitter!"

"You didn't need to. Your notebook sparkles with menace."

Rupa passed out slices of banana bread. Mo began sketching something quietly on the back of a receipt. Lee fixed a chair leg no one had noticed was broken. Sam sat back and looked around at her gloriously dysfunctional crew.

And for the first time all week, she exhaled.

Not in defeat, but in the quiet, contented kind of way that says, "*these are my people.*"

"I've done a lot of things this week," she said, "and I still don't know what I'm actually good at."

"That's fine," said Rupa. "Most of us don't."

Mo added, without looking up, "You'll find your thing."

"Or make it up," said Tasha brightly. "I could write you a workshop. 'How Not To Volunteer... With Confidence.'"

"Call it *Flailing With Purpose*," Sam muttered.

They all laughed. Even Ronnie - just a twitch of the mouth, but it definitely counted.

Outside, the drizzle had picked up. The pavement glistened in that poetic, mildly inconvenient way. Somewhere in the distance, a dog barked at a lamppost, and a toddler screamed at a butterfly. Life, in all its chaotic glory, continued.

Sam watched the rain and clutched her tea a little tighter. She didn't have a five-year plan. Or a two-day plan. Or, let's be honest, a working printer.

But she had friends, tea, banana bread, and the ridiculous belief that if she just kept showing up, something good would come of it.

The conversation had drifted to Rupa's neighbourhood WhatsApp group - currently imploding over a Bake Sale Incident involving fondant penguins and passive-aggressive emojis.

Sam sipped her tea and made a decision.

"Right," she said, sitting up. "I'm not giving up. I'm going to try again next week."

Lee looked over. "Why?"

Sam smiled. "Because I think I'm on the edge of something good."

Tasha smiled in her special way. "Let's all try something next week. Together."

Ronnie didn't even turn around. "Kettle's on. You'll need it."

And just like that, the most unofficial, unqualified, utterly chaotic community group in town was born.

Not with a bang.

But with a banana loaf, a busted chair leg, and one very determined, tea-fuelled tree.

Litter Picking and Teddy Bear Rescues

Sam had never felt more hopeful about a task that involved bin bags.

After a week of being barked at by Nigel the chihuahua, misclassifying custard, triggering a dessert-based insurrection, and falling backwards off a stage while portraying a tree with mild commitment issues, she needed something simple.

Something safe.

Something that didn't involve dramatic children, flammable props, or anyone accusing her of being "emotionally deciduous."

Enter litter picking.

It sounded ideal. Peaceful. Purposeful. Outdoorsy - but not in the terrifying "wear breathable layers and carry Kendal Mint Cake" sort of way. More "fresh air and low expectations," which was very much her niche.

The email had read:

"Just show up at the community centre at 9 a.m. We'll provide gloves, pickers, and bags. All welcome!"

Sam had mentally added:

No toddlers. No Nigel. No papier-mâché. No chance of accidentally setting fire to the future of the youth.

She arrived in joggers, a hoodie, and what she hoped were waterproof trainers, though they may have just been optimism with laces. The community centre car park was half full, mostly with people who looked like they'd been born in a fleece. They had thermos flasks. Possibly even emergency flapjacks. They looked like the kind of people who owned weather-appropriate coats.

A cheerful woman named Elaine handed her a picker stick and a hi-vis vest that smelled of wet nylon and gave the sense of slightly repressed dreams.

"Grab a bag and start wherever," Elaine said. "Mind the brambles. And the foxes. We think they're starting a gang."

Sam nodded, adjusted her vest, and set off.

The first fifteen minutes were weirdly therapeutic.

One crushed cola can. One crisp packet performing a tiny drama in the breeze. Two receipts, three bottle caps, and an object that might've been part of a shoe - or possibly a toaster from 1984. Sam didn't ask. It felt rude.

It was quiet. Gloriously so.

No dogs. Just the soft whoosh of distant cars and a very opinionated bird yelling its manifesto from a tree.

And then she saw it.

The teddy.

It sat nestled in a bush like a forgotten relic from someone's childhood or a very niche horror film. One ear drooped mournfully. The fur was a bit matted. Its eyes stared in different directions. It wore a tiny green jumper, slightly frayed, with the word *Snuggle* stitched across the front in faded thread.

Sam froze. Tilted her head.

"Oh no," she whispered. "You have a backstory, don't you?"

She bent down with her picker stick, lifted the bear gently into the bag... and paused.

Could you throw away something that clearly once meant everything to someone?

This wasn't just litter. This was heartbreak with buttons.

"I'm not okay," she told the bear quietly, "but I'm here. So... that's something."

A car honked in the distance. A Tesco receipt slapped her in the face with all the grace of an unpaid bill. The bear looked up from inside the bag with silent, fluffy judgement.

She sat down on a low wall, picker stick across her knees, the bear beside her like a tiny life coach in knitwear. The sky was grey. The world felt paused.

Her brain, being her brain, drifted.

Lately, her life had felt like a handbag in need of emptying. Cluttered. Sticky. Full of useful things she couldn't quite reach, and rogue crumbs from past decisions.

Was she doing anything useful? Or just flinging herself into chaos with good intentions and bad aim?

Was she even wearing waterproof trousers, or just very ambitious leggings?

Her phone buzzed.

Mo: "How's the litter situation?"

Sam: "I may have adopted a bear."

Mo: "This seems both concerning and inevitable."

She took a photo of the bear perched on the wall, ears floppy, jumper slightly askew, like a small protestor on a picket line of lost toys. She sent it to the group chat.

Tasha: "Look at its little jumper!"

Rupa: "Is it clean? I can wash it. I have industrial-strength Dettol."

Lee: "Missing an ear? I can fix that."

Sam smiled.

She finished her route. The picker now felt like an extension of her arm - a weirdly empowering claw of purpose. Her bag filled with the debris of human life: one single Croc (left foot), a mug that said *World's Okayest Dad*, and what she was fairly sure was a melted dinosaur, or possibly a failed candle experiment.

She returned to the car park, arms sore, legs aching, heart... lighter?

Elaine handed her a sticker that said COMMUNITY HERO and a mini roll that had clearly been sat on at some point.

Sam tucked the bear under her arm like a small, judgmental handbag and headed home.

That evening, back at Perk Up Café, the bear was placed gently on the table like an offering to the gods of whimsy.

"He needs a name," Sam announced.

"Barry," said Mo.

"No, I already have a plant called Barry. They might fight."

"Trevor Junior," suggested Tasha, as if it had always been obvious.

"That feels spiritually correct."

Lee, without a word, got out his sewing kit and began reattaching the bear's ear. Rupa rummaged through her bag and produced some leftover sock yarn to knit a tiny scarf.

From behind the counter, Ronnie watched the scene unfold and shook their head. "You lot are dangerously close to becoming wholesome."

Sam sat back, Trevor Junior beside the sugar bowl like a tiny mascot of gentle defiance, and felt something she hadn't felt in a long while.

Pride.

Not the big, showy kind. Not the "look-at-me" type with hashtags and filtered selfies.

Just the quiet kind.

The kind that comes from showing up. From doing something small, silly, simple. From picking up what others had dropped and holding it gently instead of throwing it away.

"Today," Sam whispered to the bear, "you were rescued. And so was I. Just a bit."

Ronnie sighed, topped up everyone's mugs with a performative eyeroll, and muttered, "If any of you try to knit that bear a hat, I'm confiscating the sugar."

And no one said it, but they all knew Sam had found something good. Not glittery. Not perfect.

But good.

Bingo, Biscuits and Brutal Honesty

It was Rupa's idea.

Which, in Sam's experience, was usually the start of something questionable. Rupa had a warm heart, a generous spirit, and a deeply troubling optimism about what Sam could reasonably be expected to survive.

"It'll be fun!" she'd said. "Local bingo night. They need a caller. You've got a great voice!"

"My voice sounds like a kettle having a breakdown during rush hour," Sam had replied.

"Nonsense. You're perfect."

And because Sam was a recovering people-pleaser with questionable boundaries and a fondness for chaos disguised as community spirit, she'd said yes.

Which is how, at 6:55 p.m. on a damp Thursday, Sam found herself standing on a tiny stage at the back of the local community hall - a room that smelled of decades of tea, Werther's Originals, and something vaguely floral but visually threatening.

The crowd was seated. And they were ready.

Not just any crowd. No.

Pensioners.

Not the cuddly, cardigan-wearing ones you see on telly.

These were the real ones. The steel-nerved, handbag-wielding, dabber-clutching veterans of the bingo battlefield.

They sat in silent rows, grouped by allegiance, eyes sharp, dabbers loaded. There was murmuring. There was tension. One woman was polishing her spectacles with the kind of precision only used in high-stakes surgery.

Sam clutched the bingo roller like it might turn into a weapon.

Margaret - tonight's organiser, not to be confused with Food Bank Margaret - offered a smile.

"Just read the numbers clearly, don't go too fast, and absolutely don't mess up B12."

Sam blinked. "What's wrong with B12?"

From the front row, a woman in a paisley blouse slowly turned her head. Her perm was formidable. Her aura was ex-headmistress meets MI5.

"You'll find out," she said.

Sam nodded and internally whispered, *Oh no.*

She stepped up to the mic, cleared her throat, and tried not to sound like a frightened squirrel.

"Good evening, everyone! Eyes down, dobbers ready... Let's play bingo!"

Polite applause. One cough. A sniff that may or may not have been a threat.

The first few numbers were a hit.

"Two little ducks - twenty-two!"

"A cup of tea - number three!"

A couple of chuckles. A man in the third row muttered, "She's no Gloria, but she'll do."

Sam smiled. Maybe, just maybe, this wasn't going to end in tears or a tribunal.

Then... B12.

"One and two - B12!" she called.

The room froze.

From Table Six, Paisley Blouse stood. Not fully - just enough to radiate authority.

"WRONG!"

Sam nearly swallowed the microphone.

"That's twelve. B12 is its own thing. It stands alone."

Someone gasped. A man hissed. Another dramatically dobbed the number and muttered, "Well that's my night ruined."

"I - I'm sorry," Sam stammered. "Still learning!"

"You should be."

From the back, Rupa wildly gestured the universal sign for move on before they start an uprising.

Sam did. Sort of. She skipped N33, accidentally called G47 twice, and dropped three balls under the table - one of which was never seen again, having mysteriously vanished into someone's handbag. Possibly accidental. Possibly theft. Hard to tell.

By the end of the night, Sam was mentally wrung out and pretty sure she'd been disqualified from Table Six.

She stepped down to tepid applause.

A man gave her a thumbs up.

A woman from Table Four handed her a Fox's biscuit and said gently, "You tried, love. That's more than most."

Paisley Blouse approached. Sam braced.

"You've got potential," she said, arms folded like an origami swan made of disapproval. "But next time, don't improvise. This is bingo, not jazz."

Sam nodded solemnly. "Understood."

Back at the café, the gang - now unofficially known as The Saturday Survivors - were already deep in their usual analysis of tea temperature and Ronnie's emotional state.

Sam flopped into her seat.

"They booed you?" Mo asked, wide-eyed.

"It was more of a low growl. But yes."

"I got scolded for jazz-based bingo delivery."

Tasha clapped her hands. "I'd pay to hear that! 'Next up, a moody little number we call... sixty-four.'"

Rupa passed her a biscuit. "They gave you feedback via shortbread. That's incredibly efficient. At home we don't do subtle - my aunt just slides a plate of samosas at you and tells you you've messed up. It's basically edible feedback."

"Ethel from Table Six said I have the voice of a traffic warden."

"She's not wrong," said Lee, not looking up from fixing the café's wobbly saltshaker. "You do go a bit... stern when you panic."

"I rhymed seventeen with spaghetti spleen."

Silence.

Then Tasha let out a scream-laugh and snorted tea up her nose.

Ronnie arrived, arms folded, full unimpressed café mafia mode activated.

"Let me guess. Chaos?"

"I triggered bingo-related trauma around vitamin supplements."

Ronnie sighed. "You going back?"

Sam paused. "Yeah. I think I am. But I'm bringing biscuits. A peace offering. Possibly a bribe."

69

Ronnie slid a packet of shortbread across the counter like it was a weapon.

"Tell Table Six they're from someone who also doesn't tolerate nonsense."

Sam clutched the biscuits like they were holy relics.

"Thanks. I think I'm finally getting the hang of this."

Ronnie smirked. "Or at least learning how to survive it."

Sam looked at the biscuits, then the group, then the biscuit again.

She whispered, "Be strong."

Burnt Out but Still Curious

By Saturday morning, Sam had what she liked to call *"volunteer fatigue"* - also known as emotional whiplash with a side of biscuit crumbs and a faint sense of identity loss.

She'd tried eight different roles in two weeks.

Worn five separate name badges.

Been chased by a dog the size of a handbag but with the wrath of a Greek god.

Mislabelled custard and insulted a pensioner's bingo legacy.

Oh, and accidentally started a conversation about alien infiltration at the post office.

She was done.

Not *"oh, I could do with a nap"* done.

Properly, soul-deep, *"if one more person says 'bless you for helping' I might cry into a packet of bourbons"* done.

So, when she stepped into the café, flopped into her regular booth like a collapsed camping chair, and stared blankly at the mug Ronnie slid across the table without a word - everyone knew.

Sam was on the edge.

Not the dramatic, cinematic kind of edge.

More the quietly frayed sort.

Rupa was the first to speak, gently, like Sam might disintegrate if startled.

"You alright, love? You look like someone told you Eastender's been discontinued."

Sam wrapped her hands around the tea like it was life support.

"I think I'm broken. My will to help others has... a puncture."

Tasha slid into the booth beside her, scarf unravelled and trailing like a poetic metaphor about losing the plot.

"Rough week?"

"I was booed by pensioners. I made a teenager cry during a sewing session because I couldn't tell if his jeans were fashionably distressed or just tragic. And I may have started a conspiracy chat with Trevor about aliens in Royal Mail."

Mo gave a thoughtful nod. "Classic Tuesday."

Sam lowered her head to the table, resting her forehead against the wood with the solemnity of someone giving up mid-parsnip at a Sunday roast.

"I don't know what I'm doing."

Lee, who was quietly fixing the sugar stand (again), replied without looking up, "None of us do."

And there it was.

That special kind of silence.

The one that only happens between friends who've all - independently and simultaneously - realised they're faking it.

Faking adulthood.

Faking control.

Faking like they haven't recently Googled *"how to fake knowing what you're doing."*

Rupa stirred her tea thoughtfully. "I've been thinking. Maybe we're looking at this all wrong."

"What, like... from the front?" Sam muttered into the table.

"No, I mean... what if instead of each of us running around trying to be useful separately, we just... do something together?"

Tasha lit up instantly, eyes sparkling like someone about to start a flash mob.

"Yes! Like a group project! A community thing! We could - "

"Don't say *'initiative,'"* Ronnie groaned from behind the counter. "I swear to God if you say *'initiative'* I'm locking the kettle."

"I'm not sure I have the energy for an initiative," Sam mumbled, sitting up slowly. She looked like she'd been physically and mentally tumble-dried.

Rupa leaned forward. "You wouldn't be doing it alone. We've all got something. Little things. What if we taught each other? Shared stuff?"

Mo frowned. "I don't have anything to teach."

"You built a shelf system from scratch," Lee pointed out.

"And a full cat costume for your niece," added Tasha.

"That was different. That was... satin-based coercion."

"You used bias binding," Tasha said, eyes wide. "You have hidden flair."

Mo sank further into his cardigan like a shy tortoise.

Sam stared into her tea like it might reveal the meaning of life.

"What would I teach? How to survive public embarrassment? Disaster management with a comedic twist?"

"You're funny when you panic," Rupa said kindly.

"Thanks... I think?"

"No, seriously. You keep things moving. Even when you glue yourself to furniture."

"That happened once."

"Twice," Mo said. "If you count the café chair incident."

Ronnie cleared their throat loudly and appeared at the table with the air of someone reluctantly adopting a family of enthusiastic rabbits.

"You're not starting a class in here, are you?"

Sam blinked. "No? Maybe? I honestly don't know anymore."

Ronnie stared at them all.

Paused.

Sighed.

"Fine. But no glitter. If I have to unclog the coffee machine because someone thought sequins were *festive foam,*' I will set fire to something precious."

Sam smiled.

And for the first time all week, something in her shoulders let go.

It wasn't a plan.

It wasn't an initiative.

It definitely wasn't a well-funded community programme with laminated leaflets and a logo.

But it was *something*.

A flicker. A maybe.

Maybe, despite everything - the chaos, the biscuit diplomacy, the empathy tea - she wasn't the only one trying to feel useful.

Maybe they were all just different shapes of lost, bumping into each other in the same café and pretending not to be.

She looked around the table:

- Rupa, queen of banana bread.
- Mo, silent genius with a flair for fabric.
- Tasha, walking theatre production with a scarf-based filing system.
- Lee, the quiet fix-it guy who noticed everything.

"I don't think volunteering's meant to feel like this," Sam said softly. "But... I still feel like I'm on the edge of something good."

Tasha grinned. "Let's try it. Let's all have a go. What's the worst that could happen?"

Ronnie rolled their eyes so hard it could've powered a small town.

"You start a club. You teach a class. Someone misuses the microwave, and it explodes. Again."

Mo perked up. "That wasn't me."

"I know it was Sam," Ronnie said, without looking.

Sam raised both hands in mock surrender.

"It was a cheese toastie. It was an experiment in edible optimism!"

Ronnie poured another round of tea and muttered, "Just try not to set fire to anyone. Or anything."

Sam looked at the group - the glorious mess of them.

The accidental tribe formed from chaos and caffeine.

They weren't forming a committee.

Or starting a revolution.

Or saving the world.

But maybe - just maybe - they were beginning something.

A place to show up.

To mess up.

To laugh.

To learn.

To try.

Even if all it led to was one more burnt toastie and a lot more tea.

She lifted her mug in a quiet, hopeful toast.

"To community."

"To catastrophe," said Tasha, raising her napkin.

"To bias binding," whispered Mo.

"To fixing things," added Lee.

Ronnie walked past and muttered, "To clearing glitter from the grout."

Sam smiled.

It wasn't perfect.

It wasn't polished.

But it was *theirs*.

Café Confessions

The Skills Audit (with Cake)

The meeting wasn't officially a meeting.

It was Saturday.

They were in a café.

There was cake.

And yet... they also had coloured pens, a notepad with purpose, and the unmistakable energy of something about to spiral into a project.

Tasha had arrived first, wielding a pencil case with the conviction of a woman who once led a corporate icebreaker involving tambourines.

Rupa followed, balancing a tray of banana loaf like it was a holy relic.

Sam brought flapjack. And anxiety.

Mo came with his usual cardigan and a faint air of please don't make me lead anything.

Lee had a toolkit. No one asked why. He always did.

Ronnie, behind the counter, banged the kettle like it had insulted their ancestors.

Sam uncapped a highlighter with a dramatic sigh.

"Right," she said. "Skills audit."

Ronnie snorted. "Oh no. Here we go."

81

Mo frowned. "Audit sounds... formal. Like someone's about to revoke our biscuits."

"We're not being marked," Tasha said, drawing a rainbow across the top of the page. "We're being witnessed. By the universe."

"Okay," Rupa said, unwrapping the banana loaf and placing it in the middle of the table. "Then let's not call it an audit. Let's call it... Show and Tell. For grown-ups. But with more carbs."

"Better," Lee agreed, already eyeing the loaf like it might solve all of his problems.

Sam cleared her throat. "What are we all good at?"

Silence.

Awkward, twitchy, everyone-staring-at-the-table silence.

The kind where nobody wants to sound arrogant, but also no one wants to admit they feel like a walking IKEA instruction manual - slightly unclear and missing key parts.

"Rupa," Sam said, pointing. "You're up first."

Everyone already knew Rupa could cook, of course.

She'd grown up in a kitchen where recipes were told, not written - her mum waving jars of spice like they were punctuation. To Rupa, feeding people was shorthand for love, whether it was a careful dal at home or banana bread cobbled together for the group. She blushed whenever anyone called it a "skill," but the way her food quieted a room said enough.

"I don't really have any skills," Rupa began, immediately lying through her cardigan.

"You made dinner for six using lentils, breadcrumbs, and sheer willpower," Mo said.

"And turned it into a TED Talk about food waste," added Lee.

"You label your fridge shelves," said Tasha, with something close to awe.

Rupa shrugged. "I guess I can cook. I like feeding people. I can stretch a meal for five into a meal for twelve with a tin of tomatoes and a bag of lentils. My mum never measured spices, just waved the tin and said, 'trust your nose.' Which is great until you sneeze into a pan of cumin seeds."

Sam wrote:

Rupa – Cooking, food magic, domestic planning wizard.

"Excellent. Next Tasha?"

Tasha was drama school through and through - scarf, stage presence, and the ability to turn even a tea break into a dress rehearsal.

People sometimes slowed their words with her, or assumed she'd fade into the background.

Instead, she leaned forward, full of spark, turning every pause into a scene and every glance into connection. She didn't see "different," she saw material. Every moment was raw material for a performance, every conversation a chance to make someone feel seen.

For Tasha, theatre wasn't about applause, it was about connection - and she had a knack for reminding the others that showing up with heart mattered more than getting the lines perfect.

"That's easy," Tasha beamed. "Drama. Movement. Team building. Making people cry through interpretive dance."

Sam, barely blinking, wrote:

Tasha – Performance, public speaking, eco-emotion theatre.

Tasha added a star next to her name and underlined it in glitter pen. Twice.

"Mo?"

Mo was happiest in the background, needle in hand, quietly stitching order into the world while everyone else made noise. Tall, softly spoken, and sharp-eyed, he'd grown up in a house where mending was second nature - his gran refused to throw anything away if it could be patched, hemmed, or fixed. That rubbed off on him.

He didn't chase the spotlight; he preferred steady work, quiet care, and letting the finished repair speak for itself.

"I sew. Sometimes. Quietly."

"You made an entire nativity costume set from scraps," Rupa reminded him.

"Your donkey ears were architecturally sound," Sam added.

Mo mumbled something about structural integrity and vanished into his cardigan.

Mo – Sewing, repairs, stealth excellence.

"Lee?"

Lee had the kind of mind that saw broken things and immediately pictured how to put them right. People sometimes mistook his silence for distance, but really he was just processing - spotting angles, patterns, fixes before anyone else had even noticed the problem.

Most of what he knew came from hours spent on YouTube, absorbing tutorials the way other people binged box sets. Hinges, sockets, lamps, tables - if it wobbled or flickered, Lee had probably already worked out the solution.

He didn't talk much, and he never asked for credit, but his repairs carried his signature: quiet, precise, and done before you'd realised he'd started.

He glanced toward the door like it might offer escape.

"I... fix stuff. I've got tools. I like mending things. Quietly."

"You fixed my chair with three screws and pure determination," said Sam.

"He fixed the coffee machine too," called Ronnie, still eavesdropping.

"That wasn't broken!" Sam yelled. "It was just... technologically unstable!"

Lee – Fixing, building, silent heroism, glitter-avoidance.

Then all eyes turned to Sam.

She looked up, startled. "What?"

"What are you good at?" Rupa asked.

"I - " Sam paused. "I make things worse. But... entertainingly."

"You got us all here," Rupa said.

"You start things," Mo offered.

"You talk to people," said Lee. "Even the really grumpy ones."

"You make chaos feel like an event," Tasha grinned.

Sam blinked.

Then, slowly, she wrote:

Sam – Chaos management, without instruction manuals.

With a bit of an edit, the page now read:

- Rupa: cooking, meal magic, rationing expertise
- Tasha: performance, movement, storytelling
- Mo: sewing, repairs, calm under glitter
- Lee: fixing, building, quiet mentoring
- Sam: chaos control, tea, spontaneous leadership

She stared at it.

It wasn't a strategy.

Or a grant proposal.

Or even a proper to-do list.

But it was something.

And that something felt more real than anything she'd written since applying for a job titled *Assistant to the Interim Resource Consultant* and immediately crying into a Pret sandwich.

Ronnie arrived with fresh mugs.

"What's this, then?" they asked, glancing at the paper.

"We're listing our skills," Sam explained.

Ronnie squinted. "What for? Swapping them like Pokémon cards?"

There was a pause.

"Actually…" said Tasha slowly.

Sam leaned forward. "That's… not the worst idea."

"We could teach each other," Rupa said. "No pressure. Just see what happens. One little thing at a time."

"No forms?" asked Mo.

"No glitter contracts?" begged Lee.

Ronnie groaned. "If this turns into a team-building activity I will throw someone into the compost bin."

Mo picked up a pen. "I'll bring my sewing machine."

Lee nodded. "I've got spare pliers."

Rupa beamed. "And I'll bake. Obviously."

Sam looked at the list again. Then at her friends. Then at the café - chipped mugs, sticky menus, slightly wonky chairs.

It wasn't much.

But it was something.

It was *starting*.

"Alright then," she said. "Let's swap some skills."

Ronnie, retreating behind the counter, muttered, "God help us all."

But the kettle hissed.

The pens were uncapped.

The banana loaf had mysteriously disappeared.

And somewhere between the glitter pens and the teacups... a new kind of community was quietly brewing.

Thread, Toast, and Tension

Mo didn't want to run a sewing session.

He said yes the way people say yes to helping someone move house in the rain. Or drive to Luton Airport at 3 a.m. There was a sigh, a wince, and the air of a man already regretting his past decisions.

So, when Saturday rolled around and the café's table was cleared of crumbs and dignity, Mo arrived clutching a small sewing machine, a tub of fabric scraps, and the haunted look of someone who'd rather be swallowed whole by a patchwork beanbag.

"You don't have to teach," Sam said, watching him plug in with the cautious reverence of someone setting up a lie detector. "Just share. No syllabus. No pressure. No PowerPoint. Just... vibes."

Mo nodded slowly. "Vibes I can do."

Tasha turned up next, swept dramatically in, and dropped a carrier bag on the table.

"I brought my trousers."

There was a beat.

"They've got a rip," she added, indicating the sort of tear that might get you arrested in certain churches.

Sam squinted. "That wasn't there yesterday."

"I fell."

"On what? A rake?"

"I was creating a learning opportunity," Tasha said, like she worked in HR for chaos.

Mo stared at the trousers. "You want me to fix those?"

"I want you to fix them while I learn," Tasha said, already pulling out a notepad.

Rupa arrived with toast.

Not just any toast - artisan sourdough, golden and crisped, with banana slices aligned like a crop circle made by a very hungry alien.

She placed it in front of Mo with gentle solemnity. "For strength. And potassium."

Lee showed up, toolbox in hand, despite having nothing to fix. It was just how he travelled. Like others bring wine to a dinner party, Lee brought adjustable spanners to a conversation.

Sam, meanwhile, was attempting to thread a needle and whispering threats under her breath.

"I swear to every deity, if you don't let me through your stupid little eye, I will throw you into a black hole."

Mo took it off her gently, threaded it in three seconds flat, and passed it back without a word. Just a look. The look of a man who fixes things. And judges you.

"Right," he said. "We're starting with cushion covers."

Sam lit up. "I love cushions."

"Great," said Mo. "Let's try making one that doesn't look like it's been compromised."

"Wow. Harsh but fair."

The session began. Mo showed them how to cut fabric without summoning demons. Tasha got distracted designing a cape. Rupa kept feeding people toast like she was running for Local Saint of the Year. Lee fixed a chair no one had reported broken. Ronnie, pretending to reorganise teabags, was 100% eavesdropping.

Sam stitched two squares together with the intensity of a bomb technician. Her tongue poked out. Her stitches wobbled like anxiety on a rollercoaster.

"I think my cushion's having an emotional episode," she said, holding up something vaguely square and extremely... textured.

Rupa smiled supportively. "It's got depth."

"It looks like it's seen war," said Lee.

"I think it just whispered, 'help me,'" said Tasha.

Mo laughed. A quiet, real laugh. Possibly his first of the day. It was like hearing a cat purr. Unexpected. Deeply rewarding.

By the end of the session:

- Rupa had repaired one of her niece's toy rabbits (the rabbit now looked both grateful and slightly traumatised).

- Tasha had turned her trousers into a patchwork skirt described as "avant-garde" by everyone who didn't want to be sued.

- Sam's cushion resembled a survivor. But a proud one.

- Lee had fixed a lamp that no one had brought - it was just... there. Probably broken.

- Mo looked shattered. But in that "I've done a good thing and now need toast and a lie-down" kind of way.

Ronnie appeared holding a suspicious roll of tape and a face that said they were about to do something they'd immediately regret.

"You lot are going to ask for more space, aren't you?"

Sam blinked. "What kind of space?"

"The table at the back. The one under the passive-aggressive motivational poster and near the plug socket that only works if you believe in it."

Tasha perked up like someone had just announced surprise biscuits. "Could we?"

Ronnie sighed. The long-suffering kind. The kind that only comes from years of caffeine, chaos, and once having to explain to a grown man that fairy lights are not legal tender.

"Fine. It's yours. Permanently. Reserved. For whatever this is that you're doing. Skill swapping. Emotional knitting. But there are rules."

They held up one finger. "No glitter."

Another. "No tap dancing without prior written consent."

A third. "No starting a cult. Even a small one."

"No promises," Sam muttered.

Ronnie turned to go, then paused. "Mo. Good job today."

Mo blinked. It was possibly the most Ronnie had ever said to him. Certainly the nicest.

They packed up slowly. Folded fabric. Finished the tea. Ate the last of the toast (of course Tasha had hidden the good bit under a flyer). Sam placed her slightly wonky cushion in the centre of the now-theirs table like a proud, lumpy mascot.

"It's not perfect," she said, smoothing a crumb from the corner.

"But it's got heart," Mo replied, tapping the wood like it might start purring.

Ronnie called from the counter, "And crumbs. Everything in here's got crumbs."

They laughed.

And in the quiet that followed - amid the threads, the doodled napkins, the faint scent of ambition and banana peel - something shifted. Not just cushions. Not just routines.

But something shared.
Something sturdy.
A table-shaped kind of belonging.

Cooking for the Confused

"Welcome to chaos," said Rupa, flinging open the door to her kitchen like a glamorous ringmaster announcing the world's least-qualified cooking troupe.

Sam entered first, carrying nothing but goodwill, a wobbly sense of optimism, and a pair of swimming goggles.

Mo followed, solemn and silent, with a stack of neatly labelled Tupperware.

Lee brought a wooden spoon in his back pocket. No explanation. No one asked.

Tasha, naturally, had an apron that read *Drama Queen in Residence* and the energy of a woman ready to turn lunch into a dress rehearsal.

The mission? Cook.

Or, more specifically learn to cook without anyone setting fire to the curtains or bruising a root vegetable.

"Today's menu," Rupa declared, slapping a slightly smudged recipe card onto the counter, "is Shepherd's pie. Classic. Cheap. Comforting. Very hard to mess up."

Sam squinted. "You've met us, right?"

"I've already peeled something," Tasha announced, holding up what may once have been a carrot but now looked like a sad crayon.

"I peeled too," said Mo quietly. "It was… therapeutic."

"I peeled and chopped," said Lee. "Also reorganised your spice rack."

Rupa spun. "You what?"

"You absolute monster."

The kitchen was warm, crammed, and smelled like onions and nerves. Rupa moved through it with the authority of a dinner lady with secrets. She barked instructions like, "That's not browning, that's sulking!" and "You don't stir mince, you encourage it!"

Sam, already in her goggles, stood over an onion with an air of determination on her face.

"You're not scuba diving," said Tasha, spoon in hand.

"I cry at onions," Sam replied. "This is trauma prevention."

"You look like a sad frog preparing for surgery."

"Safety first."

Meanwhile, Lee was taking mash responsibility very seriously. Perhaps too seriously.

"Do we really need that much butter?" Sam asked.

Lee didn't blink. "It's not butter. It's loyalty."

Mo stirred his pan like it had just confided in him. Tasha chucked in a sprig of something green and dramatic.

"Just to add mystery," she said.

All was vaguely under control.

Then the smoke alarm lost its mind.

"OH MY GOD WHAT DID I DO?" Sam shouted, launching her spoon like a flailing wand of doom.

"It's not you," Rupa said, leaping across the kitchen like someone who's fought fires with flannels before. "It's Lee."

Lee was fanning the oven, looking entirely unrepentant. "I was grilling the top. For crispiness."

"You've grilled it into the afterlife!"

Sam opened a window. Mo opened a cupboard. Tasha, for reasons unclear, began singing *Total Eclipse of the Tart*.

Eventually, the alarm shut up. The pie survived. Mostly.

They served it anyway - slightly wonky, proudly scorched, topped with mashed potato that had... character.

They sat around Rupa's table, bowls in hand, steam rising, faces glowing with equal parts pride and relief.

"Wow," said Sam, taking a bite. "This tastes like school dinners - but the good kind. The kind that made Tuesdays worth it."

Mo nodded. "It's like a warm hug from someone who pays taxes and gives good advice."

"It tastes like the childhood I deserved," said Tasha, drowning hers in ketchup.

Rupa beamed. "You made this."

Just then, Ronnie appeared in the doorway holding a tray of apple crumble with all the subtlety of a *Bake Off* judge crashing a hen party.

"You came?" Sam asked.

"I didn't trust any of you not to season things with glitter," Ronnie replied, placing the tray down. "I brought pudding. Just in case."

"I used thyme," Tasha muttered.

They ate. They laughed. They passed spoons, second helpings, and unspoken compliments. And in that tiny, crumb-covered kitchen, something warm settled - a little voice saying, *You did this. Together.*

Later, Sam stood at the sink still wearing the goggles, because by then they'd become part of her personality.

"You know," she said to Rupa, "this might be the first time I've cooked something without setting off a fire extinguisher or starting a crisis."

Rupa handed her a tea towel. "You just needed the right ingredients."

Sam rolled her eyes. "That's dangerously metaphorical."

Rupa smiled. "Everything is."

Budgeting for Biscuits

Nobody expected Lee to volunteer for anything involving group attention, let alone lead a session.

Least of all Lee.

So, when he quietly said, "I could... do one on budgeting, I guess," over a particularly strong mug of tea and a slice of banana bread, the café table fell silent.

Sam blinked. "Wait. Like... budgeting-budgeting? With maths?"

Lee shrugged. "I like spreadsheets."

"You also once refused to split a dinner bill because someone didn't eat the garlic bread," Tasha said.

"It's about principles," Lee muttered.

"Do you colour-code?" Tasha asked, eyes gleaming.

Lee blinked. "Of course I colour-code."

Mo gave a solemn nod. "Respect."

And that's how, one slightly overcast Saturday, they found themselves gathered in the back of Perk Up Café, each armed with a pen, a biscuit, and a vague sense of impending fiscal enlightenment.

It was time to enter:

The Budget Zone.

"Right," said Lee, clearing his throat like he was about to announce tax reform, "we'll start with the basics. Incomings, outgoings. I've made templates."

He handed them out like a man who had absolutely practised this in front of a mirror.

Sam gasped. "Lee... these are beautiful."

Rupa nodded. "It's got tabs. I trust tabs."

Tasha had brought glitter glue.

"I thought we could decorate!" she beamed, already outlining her rent column in silver swirls.

Lee looked like he might cry. "Glitter is not a recognised financial category."

"It is if it's self-care."

"Your landlord is going to think you've joined a mystical cult of stationery."

"I have," said Tasha. "It's called 'Not Crying While Doing Maths'."

Mo was already shading his budget like a heat map. Orange for panic. Blue for bills. Green for "snacks that make me feel alive."

Sam leaned over hers. "Where do I put 'Impulse Online Purchase While Sad at 1 a.m.'?"

"Discretionary," Lee answered, without even looking up.

Rupa tapped her pen. "Does baking equipment count as expenses?"

"Yes," Sam said, "Also technically assets."

Ronnie wandered past with a tray of teas and squinted at the scene. "This looks dangerously close to personal development."

Sam grinned. "We're empowering ourselves financially."

"You're sticking sequins to a pie chart."

"It's interactive learning."

Ronnie rolled their eyes and walked off, muttering something about needing hazard pay and a glitter ban.

But the session went on.

Lee explained interest rates using a custard cream analogy.

Mo created a second sheet labelled "Emergency Button Fund" (for actual buttons... and also when life unbuttons you a bit).

Tasha discovered she'd been emotionally investing in scented candles and categorised them as "wellbeing – dramatic tier."

Rupa worked out how much she spent on pasta. The answer was... enlightening.

By the end, every person around the table had a customised, glitter-sprinkled, slightly crumb-covered budget plan - and a new appreciation for the quiet power of a man who brings a calculator to a café and means it.

"You're really good at this," Sam said as Lee gathered his immaculate handouts with the reverence of a monk folding sacred parchment.

He shrugged. "I used to panic about money. So, I made a system. Then the system became a habit."

"And now it's a spreadsheet?"

Lee gave a tiny smile. A spreadsheet smile.

"Now it's control."

Rupa slid a flapjack across the table like an ancient ritual offering. "You're a quiet marvel."

"I'm really not."

"You really are."

He turned bright red and stared into his empty mug like it might rescue him.

Tasha waved her glitter pen. "We should run this again. Budgeting for biscuits. Candle inflation. Shopping regrets. You could tour it."

"I don't want to tour."

"Mini tour?"

"No."

"Spreadsheets & Snacks?"

"...Still no."

Sam grinned. "He's blushing. That's a yes."

Just then, Ronnie reappeared and snatched the glitter pen from Tasha's hand.

"If I find sparkle in the loose tea again, you're all banned."

They laughed. Cleared up the paper, pens, and biscuit carnage.

Sam watched as Lee gently folded the spare budget sheets and tucked them into a file with deliberate, practised care.

She said softly, "You just helped five people feel less terrified of their bank statements."

Lee paused, surprised.

"That's... not nothing."

Sam smiled. "Nope. That's a superpower."

And in that quiet moment - with biscuit crumbs on the table and glitter still clinging to the air - Lee the reluctant fixer became Lee the accidental teacher.

The Drama of Recycling

Tasha had been waiting for this moment.

She'd clapped for Mo's sewing. Nodded earnestly through Lee's budget sheets. Even performed a one-woman standing ovation when Rupa produced shepherd's pie with the fire alarm only going off once. But today?

Today was hers.

"Right," she declared, dramatically flipping her scarf like it was auditioning for a part in *Les Mis: The Eco Edition*. "Today, we explore the emotional journey... of compost."

Sam, mid-sip of lukewarm tea, blinked. "Sorry. What now?"

"Recycling," Tasha said, eyes shining. "But make it theatre."

Ronnie, who happened to be passing with a tray of lemon drizzle and a deep suspicion of organised whimsy, froze mid-step. "If I see one bin lid doing a monologue, I'm locking that door and hiding the key in a quiche."

"It's educational," Tasha replied, the picture of dignity. "Also deeply moving."

"I'm already moved," muttered Mo, edging his chair closer to the wall, as if physical distance could protect him from interpretive dance.

The café's back table - recently a sewing studio, budget HQ, and minor pie-related crime scene - had been transformed into what Tasha was now calling "the drama studio." Green streamers dangled from the ceiling. A cut-out sun peeked from a cardboard cloud. In one corner sat a disturbingly realistic papier-mâché banana. Sam wasn't sure if it was meant to symbolise food waste or if Tasha had just reached a new level of sleep-deprived creativity.

"We begin," Tasha announced, standing in front of a Bluetooth speaker with the solemnity of someone about to unveil *Swan Lake: Bin Night Edition*. "With The Lifecycle of a Yogurt Pot."

Soft piano music drifted into the room. Mo visibly flinched. Rupa snorted into her tea and muttered something about "should've brought wine."

"Imagine," Tasha said, eyes wide and voice trembling with passion, "you're a single-use plastic pot. Once shiny. Now discarded."

Sam raised a hand. "Am I recyclable?"

"Emotionally? We all are."

"Fair."

Tasha launched into a heartfelt soliloquy about waste, worth, and being separated from your cardboard sleeve. She flung herself to the floor in what could generously be described as a 'dignified collapse,' whispering, "I was used."

Rupa gave a polite clap.

Mo leaned over to Sam. "Is she okay?"

"She's thriving."

Tasha sprang to her feet. "Now! Become the recycling bin!"

Sam stood up and promptly knocked into Mo.

"Sorry, I didn't realise you were becoming a compost caddy."

"I thought I was landfill," he muttered, with the solemnity of a man who has truly locked into the void of waste disposal.

"You've got main bin energy," Sam replied, trying to form herself into something bin-shaped.

Meanwhile, Rupa was reverse-beeping like a council lorry with a sinus problem. Tasha had apparently cast her in the role of 'municipal vehicle,' and Rupa was embracing it with gusto.

Then came... The Banana.

Tasha disappeared behind a curtain (actually a shower curtain from Ronnie's cupboard) and re-emerged in a full-body yellow foam costume with a tiny hat. No one asked where she got it. Everyone silently agreed they didn't want to know.

"I am organic waste," she declared. "I return to the earth. I transform. I compost."

Lee, sitting against the radiator like he was hoping to fuse with it, whispered, "I'm starting to believe it."

Mo, now playing the role of 'Confused Paper' in a group tableau, looked up as if he was more confused than the paper.

By the end of the session:

- Sam had performed a stirring piece called *The Tin Can's Lament,* which mainly involved rolling across the floor whispering, "Re... cy... cle meee..."

- Rupa narrated the inner monologue of a plastic milk bottle with an accent that may or may not have been Welsh.

- Mo reluctantly interpretive-danced the lifecycle of a crushed pizza box, wearing a headband made of cardboard.

- Lee refused to move but did fix a wonky recycling bin between scenes, stating, "This was bothering me more than your banana."

- Ronnie stood at the doorway, arms crossed, but didn't leave. Which was, for them, high praise.

They eventually collapsed into chairs. Sweaty. Slightly breathless. Emotionally... unsure.

Tasha beamed, her banana hat slightly askew. "So... how did it feel to be the recycling?"

Sam stared at her. "Philosophical?"

"Crinkly," Rupa offered.

"Damp," said Mo, inspecting his elbow.

Lee passed Sam a stray bottle cap. "It's what I imagine my brain looks like on a Thursday night."

Ronnie appeared with iced tea, because chaos always made them thirsty. "That was a lot of effort to remind people to rinse out yoghurt pots."

"Art," said Tasha, "requires commitment."

Sam took a long sip. "That was the most unhinged thing I've ever done."

"And yet," Tasha said, "you were brilliant."

"I was a tin can."

"A tragic tin can."

Sam sighed. "I feel like this group is lowering my threshold for what counts as a productive Saturday."

"And yet," Rupa said, "we all showed up. Again."

Ronnie hovered. "So, is this going to be a weekly thing now? Because if next week involves puppets, I'm calling the council."

Tasha glowed with the smug satisfaction of someone whose soul had been nourished by banana-based art. "Next week is Sam's turn."

Sam nearly dropped her cup. "My what?"

"Your skill session."

"I don't have a skill," Sam said. "Unless we're counting panic-ordering highlighters in bulk during emotional spirals."

"Maybe we are," Rupa said.

"Everyone's good at something," Tasha added, peeling off the banana suit like a snake shedding regret.

Sam groaned. "Can I just do a session on tea?"

Ronnie muttered, "You already do that daily, unofficially."

"What about time management?" suggested Lee.

"I show up 15 minutes late to everything."

"Emergency improvisation?" said Mo.

"Too real."

"Handling emotional whiplash in a banana-heavy environment?" Tasha offered helpfully.

Sam slumped. "Fine. But no costumes."

Ronnie passed by. "Wait till fridge theatre week."

Everyone froze.

"...They're joking, right?" Sam asked.

No one answered.

Rupa took a sip of tea. "I call dibs on being the expired cheese."

And somehow - in the back of a café filled with crumbs, laughter, and just the faintest whiff of banana foam - another ordinary Saturday had turned into something weird, wonderful, and unexpectedly bonding.

Just your average compost cabaret.

The Workshop Café: Unofficial and Slightly Unhinged

It started, as all revolutions rightly should, with toast crumbs and a napkin.

Not a metaphorical napkin. A literal one. Slightly crumpled. Lightly butter-stained. And currently covered in glittery doodles courtesy of Tasha, who was hunched over it like it was the Magna Carta of community craft chaos.

Sam peered over her mug. "What's that meant to be? A confused octopus in a teacup?"

Tasha didn't even flinch. "It's a logo," she declared, spinning it around with a dramatic flair that knocked over Mo's pen. "For us."

"Us?" Sam repeated, instantly suspicious.

Rupa looked up from her current knitting project - a tea cosy that resembled either a badger or a disgruntled hedgehog, depending on the angle. "Us as in...?"

"This! What we're doing! Teaching each other skills. Burning shepherd's pie. Learning budgeting from a man who colour-codes his snacks. We're a group. A thing." She gestured at the table, which was currently covered in biscuit debris, highlighters, someone's rogue sock (possibly Mo's), and at least three mugs of undrinkable tea.

"We're a vibe," Tasha added, reverently.

Mo looked up. "We're a bunch of exhausted adults trying not to cry in a café."

"Exactly," Tasha beamed. "That's branding."

The napkin, when examined, showed a hand-drawn teacup - from which protruded a needle, a whisk, a spanner, and what might've been Lee, judging by the tiny frown and an extremely realistic eyebrow.

Above it, in glitter gel pen, were three words:

The Workshop Café

There was a pause. A reverent, biscuit-munching pause.

"I... don't hate it," Sam admitted, which, from her, was akin to an enthusiastic standing ovation.

"It does sound like a dating app for people who make their own jam," said Lee.

"But also like something you'd see on a corkboard next to 'Mindful Knitting Mondays' and 'Chair Yoga for the Chronically Overcaffeinated'," added Rupa.

"It's slightly unhinged," Mo muttered.

Tasha sat back, proud as anything. "Perfect. That's us."

They all stared at the napkin. For a brief, surreal moment, it felt like it might start glowing and bestow community funding or a visit from someone with a clipboard and mild authority.

Then Sam, fuelled by toast and impulsive optimism, said, "I'll make a poster."

"No glitter!" Ronnie shouted from the counter, without even looking up.

"Agreed," said Mo, deadpan.

"Debatable," muttered Tasha, already reaching for her sparkle pens.

Sam did not take this lightly. She marched to the library, armed with too much enthusiasm and absolutely no graphic design training. What emerged several hours (and one baffled librarian) later was a poster containing:

- Seven fonts
- Four motivational quotes
- One inexplicably large teacup with googly eyes
- A QR code that didn't actually go anywhere

She jammed the printer so thoroughly that it coughed out 42 copies, all at a jaunty angle, while making a noise that sounded suspiciously like a sheep sneezing.

Undeterred, Sam returned to the café with a stack of off-kilter flyers and a grin that could power a small village.

They pinned one to the café noticeboard. Another in the community centre. One ended up in the vet's waiting room. Another got stuck in a hedge, where it was later found by a dog walker who came in asking if the group did obedience training (they did not).

Tasha handed one to a man in the park. He was power walking for charity and didn't stop, but the flyer did briefly become part of his motivational playlist.

And somehow - through sheer biscuit-fuelled determination - people noticed.

Not many. Not all at once. But slowly, the whispers started.

A young mum popped in asking about homemade baby food recipes.

A lad turned up with a broken zip and left with a repaired jacket and a biscuit.

Someone else came in, sat silently with a cup of tea, and said, "Is this the place where you learn stuff without anyone judging you?"

Ronnie, without missing a beat, handed over a mug. "Unfortunately, yes."

Sam watched from her usual seat as it all unfolded - people drifting in, some chatting, some just hovering, some scribbling weirdly specific requests on napkins.

One said, "Can teach crochet but only if you don't ask for a scarf."

Another, "Need help with my boiler. Or possibly my life."

And a third, simply, "Allergic to mushrooms and bad vibes. Want to learn to cook."

It was messy. Disorganised. Mildly chaotic. But it was happening.

One afternoon, a woman wandered in wearing a coat that looked like it had fought a washing machine and lost. She looked around the room - a strange mix of tea, craft, and accidental therapy - and said, "I saw your poster in the dentist. Didn't understand it. Came anyway."

Sam smiled. "That sounds about right."

Ronnie rolled their eyes, muttered something about starting a support group for café owners trapped in community initiatives, and then quietly refilled the biscuit tin.

And just like that... The Workshop Café became a thing.

Not a business. Not a charity. Not even an official group, really. Just a wonderfully scrappy idea born on a napkin, sticky-taped to the soul of the community.

They had:

- No funding
- No official training
- A dodgy kettle that hissed like it had secrets
- A poster that looked like it was made during a small emotional breakdown

But they also had:

- Each other
- A wall of scribbled notes and hopeful skills
- A place where it was okay to turn up late, tired, unsure, and still be handed a cuppa

And honestly?

That felt like enough.

Sam sat back one afternoon, watching someone nervously ask how to sew on a button while Tasha explained it using sock puppets and Lee handed over colour-coded instructions with military efficiency.

"Look at this," she whispered to Mo.

He glanced up. "Huh?"

"All of it. The napkin. The flyers. The fact that woman is teaching three teenagers how to make pasta in a room with no hob."

He followed her gaze, then nodded. "Madness."

"Beautiful madness."

He raised his mug. "To The Workshop Café."

"To the accidental, mildly glittery revolution."

And the kettle hissed its approval. Or possibly its death rattle. But no one cared.

A Curious Stranger and a Clogged Sink

Sam was three teas deep into her Thursday - and four questionable decisions in, if you counted the email she'd just sent with the typo *"kindest regerts"* as the sign-off - when the café door creaked open and a man poked his head around like he was considering entry to Narnia.

"Sorry," he said, slightly out of breath, "bit random. But does anyone here know how to fix a blocked sink?"

There was a pause.

A long, weighted, toast-crumb-laden pause.

Ronnie, armed with a cloth and a look that could curdle oat milk, glanced up from the counter. "Is this an actual plumbing issue or one of those hipster metaphors about drainage?"

"No, actual sink," the man replied. "My kitchen one. It's... making noises."

"What kind of noises?" Sam asked cautiously, already preparing herself for ghosts or gerbils.

He winced. "Like it's... learned language. Possibly in Latin."

"Demonic sink. Classic," said Tasha, not looking up from her notebook titled *Things That May Be Haunted But Useful*.

And then - without fanfare, hesitation, or even a finishing of his biscuit - Lee stood up.
Of course he did.

The man blinked. "You know plumbing?"

Lee shrugged. "Enough."

He didn't elaborate. Lee rarely did. His superpower was understatement. His other superpower was fixing things in a way that made you feel like you'd contributed even though you'd just handed him tea.

"I'll come too," Sam said, already grabbing her coat. "I can hand you things. Offer emotional support. Maybe scream helpfully."

Lee didn't say yes, but he didn't say no either - which in Lee-speak meant "I have accepted your presence and may even tolerate your commentary."

The stranger introduced himself on the way. Dan. Mid-thirties. Slightly baffled expression that suggested he'd lost his way in a DIY aisle once and never quite recovered.

"Saw your poster in the dentist," he explained.

Sam nodded. "Dentist is currently our most successful outreach partner. Unintentionally."

"I didn't totally get what it was."

"Neither do we," she replied cheerfully.

Dan's flat was tidy in the way that screamed *I cleaned because people were coming*, which, to be fair, he had. The sink, however, was not tidy. It was the opposite of tidy. It was gurgling in a way that suggested it had feelings, and none of them were good.

Lee crouched down, opened the cupboard beneath the sink like a bomb disposal expert, and peered inside.

Sam hovered behind him like a cross between a theatre usher and a nervous bystander.

"Is it bad?" she asked.

Lee grunted.

That could have meant anything from *I've seen worse* to *write me into your will.*

He pulled out a wrench. Turned to Sam. "Tea towel."

She handed it over like she was assisting a surgeon mid-transplant.

"What can I do?" she asked, immediately regretting it.

Lee pointed at a bowl. "Hold this. And be ready."

"Be ready for - ?"

A wet slurp. A sinister plonk.

Something landed in the bowl with a noise that suggested it had opinions.

Sam stared at it.

"...Is that a spoon?"

Lee shrugged. "Could be worse."

"Could it?"

"Could've been cabbage."

Sam made a noise that sounded like a nervous laugh trying to escape a mild trauma spiral.

Half an hour later, the sink was functional, the pipe was reattached, and the spoon was resting gently on a tea towel like it was being nursed back to health.

Dan stood watching them, awe-struck, holding a tin of shortbread like it was a trophy.

"That was... amazing," he said. "Honestly. I've been quoted £150 for that level of wizardry."

Lee packed away his wrench with the casual grace of a man who could fix your plumbing and your life if you asked nicely.

Dan turned to Sam. "So, what is this group, then? Are you like... a charity?"

"Not really."

"A business?"

She snorted. "Absolutely not."

"Do-gooders?"

Sam paused. Thought about last week's interpretive recycling theatre. The budget spreadsheets. The banana costume. The slightly-too-enthusiastic shepherd's pie fire.

"We're more like community-fuelled chaos with a side of accidental competency," she said. "And sometimes biscuits."

Dan grinned. "You lot aren't like the usual volunteers. That's a compliment."

"We'll take it."

He held out the tin of shortbread like it was sacred. "Seriously. Thank you."

Back at the café, Sam placed the tin on the table like it was treasure.

"Payment," she said, with dramatic flair.

Mo looked up. "For what?"

"For emergency plumbing and spoons from the void."

Rupa opened the lid. "These are the good ones. Chocolate stripes and everything."

Tasha gasped. "We've entered the biscuit big leagues."

Ronnie eyed them suspiciously. "What did you do?"

"We fixed a man's sink."

"You flooded a stranger's home?"

"Nope. All dry. All upright."

Ronnie narrowed their eyes. "You're all deeply worrying individuals."

Mo took a biscuit and nodded. "That means they're proud."

But they emptied their mugs anyway and didn't confiscate the tin - which, by Ronnie standards, was basically a public display of affection.

Sam leaned back, sipped her tea, and sniffed her sleeve.

"I smell like trauma and pipe grease."

"You smell like triumph," said Rupa.

"You smell like a blocked drain," said Tasha.

Sam looked around. The flyers. The napkin logo. The slightly absurd poster campaign that somehow reached a sink-based emergency. And now this, a biscuit tin full of gratitude and exactly three jam-filled ones already stolen by Mo.

"Do you think we're actually doing good?" she asked quietly.

Lee looked up, his expression unreadable as always.

"You've been doing good the whole time," he said. "You're just starting to believe it now."

Sam blinked.

"Thanks, Lee."

He nodded. "It's the biscuits. They bring out my emotional side."

Ronnie snorted. "You lot bring out my headache." But they were smiling when they said it.

And somewhere, on a freshly unclogged countertop, a spoon sat clean and quiet - the first unofficial relic of The Workshop Café's plumbing ministry.

Because every community starts somewhere.

Some start with a mission statement.

Some with a Facebook group.

But some?

They begin with a biscuit tin and a blocked sink.

Teaching Each Other, Messily

They called it a "session."

Which was brave, considering it began fifteen minutes late, featured three dead flipchart pens (all blue, all lying about it), and a five-minute debate over whether Hobnobs were essential educational resources or just a distraction with oats.

Still. It was happening.

They were teaching. To actual people. In public. With flipcharts and everything. A bold move, especially given their previous track record with glue sticks, spontaneous compost theatre, and the great glitter incident of week seven.

Sam was up first.

Her chosen topic?

Time Management for People Who Can't Remember Why They Walked Into the Kitchen.

"Hi," she began, standing at the front of the room with a smile that said *this is fine, I'm not internally screaming at all.* "I'm not an expert. But I have read at least four blogs and one inspirational fridge magnet."

Her audience included her friends (loyally half-listening), a sweet-but-bewildered new visitor named Marjorie who had wandered in looking for the WI meeting, and a teenager who may have only stayed because they'd already helped themselves to a biscuit and felt too awkward to leave.

She held up her notes.

They were colour-coded, laminated (badly), and bore a large brown watermark across the top corner where someone (possibly her, possibly fate) had spilled tea.

"Step one: lists," Sam declared. "I love lists. They make me feel productive. Even when the only thing I tick off is 'make list.'"

Mo nodded from the front row. "Deeply relatable."

"Step two: colour coding. If you can't solve your problems, at least make them look cheerful."

"Like highlighters," said Tasha, already rummaging in her bag for glitter gel pens.

Sam pressed on. "Step three: buy notebooks. As many as you like. You'll never fill them. But you'll feel ready."

"Is step four crying in the stationery aisle at WHSmith?" Tasha called out.

"No," said Sam. "That's step five. Step four is reorganising your to-do list in three different apps and then accidentally deleting it."

The remaining workshop was actually surprisingly helpful and even the teenager could be seen taking notes.

Marjorie clapped like she'd just witnessed a TED Talk by a mildly chaotic librarian.

"And finally," Sam said, "accept that time is a myth, clocks are rude, and stickers help everything."

Applause. Possibly out of joy, possibly because the session was over and no one had cried yet.

Sam sat down, slightly flushed and adrenaline-drenched.

Rupa passed her a flapjack like a post-battle ration. "That was excellent."

"I blacked out during the bit about calendars."

"That's where your power lies."

Next up was Mo.

He stood, cleared his throat, and introduced:

"Hemming Basics for the Easily Distracted."

All went well - for precisely ninety seconds - before Tasha, overcome with creative energy and possibly flapjack fumes, declared that her scarf was unfinished and began turning it into a cape mid-demo.

Lee, sensing danger, calmly moved the scissors further from her orbit.

"That's not a hem," he muttered. "That's a hazard."

Mo soldiered on, threading needles and occasionally ducking flying fabric.

By the end:

- Sam had a sleeve that no longer looked like it had been mauled by a drawer.

- The teenager had stitched their shirt pocket shut. On purpose. Sort of.

- Tasha had created something between a shawl and a cry for help.

Then it was Tasha's turn.

She stepped into the centre with all the gravity of someone about to announce she'd invented soup for the first time.

"Soup…" she began, pausing for dramatic effect, "is not just a meal. It is a journey."

Sam blinked. "Wait, I thought this was about lentil recipes?"

"Let. It. Happen," said Rupa.

And then Tasha launched.

It was a spoken-word performance slash group therapy session with vegetables. She described carrots as stoic life warriors, onions as layers of inherited trauma, and lentils as tiny legumes of resilience.

There were hand gestures. Dramatic pauses. At one point, she crouched beside a pot of imaginary stock and whispered to it like a grief counsellor.

Mo whispered, "I'll never look at minestrone the same again."

Sam whispered back, "I'm both confused and weirdly hungry."

When she finally bowed - to applause, including a slow clap from the teenager - the café fell into a stunned, leek-flavoured silence.

Ronnie, watching from the counter, broke it. "You people need adult supervision."

By the end of the afternoon, several things had happened:

- Sam's notebook was full of scribbled feedback, three soup recipes, and one note that simply read "WHY?" in red pen.

- Mo had given out three pre-threaded needles, a demonstration, and one lecture on never using fabric scissors on paper - which was aimed solely at Tasha.

- Rupa unveiled "focus cookies" - which were really just biscuits with raisins and good intentions.

- Tasha bowed three times and signed one paper napkin for the teenager, who now looked fully invested in Soup As Art.

And then, as they were packing up, Marjorie turned to Sam.

She reached for her hand, patted it gently, and said, "Can I come back next week?"

Sam, still unsure whether this counted as a class or a social experiment, nodded.

"Only if you bring soup."

Marjorie beamed. "Minestrone."

Tasha gasped. "My influence is spreading."

Ronnie groaned, but there was a hint of a smile behind it.

And somewhere, under the scattered biscuits and thread scraps, under the slightly charred smell of ambition and PowerPoint dreams, something had shifted.

They weren't just a group anymore.

They were a learning curve.

A beautifully chaotic, hand-hemmed, soup-fuelled learning curve.

And next week?

Next week was going to involve glue guns.

Heaven help them all.

Ronnie's Offer

Ronnie didn't do speeches. They did tea - strong enough to resuscitate a fainting goat - and sarcasm sharp enough to trim hedges. They ran the café like a warship, complete with the occasional cannon blast in the form of a sigh so heavy it could knock a latte off the counter.

So, when they cleared their throat - midway through Mo explaining why seam allowances were "basically boundaries" - it wasn't for dramatic effect. It was because something monumental was coming. Or possibly someone had spilled glitter again.

Sam looked up, hands raised in immediate self-defence. "We didn't touch the teapot this time."

"Yet," Ronnie said, with all the menace of a bouncer who's seen one too many hen parties.

Without another word, they marched past them and headed towards 'The Door'.

You know the one. The door at the back of the café, wedged between the broom cupboard and what they suspected was a haunted fuse box.

The door marked **'Staff Only – NO EXCEPTIONS'**, in capital letters and underlined twice.

The door none of them had dared to open, partly out of respect, mostly out of fear that it might lead to a different dimension - or worse, a staff appraisal.

Ronnie unlocked it with the ceremonial grunt of someone who had kept this moment in their back pocket for decades, stepped aside like a very caffeinated Gandalf.

"Go on, then. Have a look."

Cautiously, they approached. Peered in. And immediately wished they'd brought a torch. Or a priest.

It was a room. Technically.

Roughly the size of an ambitious cupboard. It smelt like old paint, dead hopes, and possibly cheese. The floor was dusty. The walls were doing that special kind of flake only paint from the 1970s can achieve.

A table sat drunkenly in the middle, held up by one brave coaster. There were three mismatched chairs, a filing cabinet of sorts, and something that might have once been a rubber plant, now resembling an abandoned wig on stilts.

Rupa sneezed. Twice.

Mo stared at the cushion in the corner. "Something just moved. I swear it blinked."

Tasha gasped, arms spread wide like she was greeting an ancient ruin. "It's perfect."

Sam tilted her head. "Is that a dead plant or… an ex-mascot?"

"Used to be the storeroom," Ronnie said, arms folded, face unreadable. "Now it's just… this. I was going to turn it into a wine cellar. Then I remembered I don't like wine, and cellars are for people who say 'summer house' unironically."

Lee squinted. "Why are you showing us this?"

Ronnie let out a sigh so long it echoed off the dodgy skirting board. "Because you lot clearly need space. Somewhere to stitch, sob over budgeting spreadsheets, and perform your weird compost theatre without scaring the paying customers."

There was a beat. The kind of silence that usually precedes a proposal or an accidental fire.

"You mean…" Sam began cautiously.

"I'm saying," said Ronnie, already regretting everything, "you can use it."

Rupa's eyes widened. "Really?"

"If you clean it. And I mean actually clean it. Not just move the dirt to significant corners. And absolutely - ABSOLUTELY - no glitter. I catch so much as a sparkle and I'm calling pest control."

Tasha's hands twitched. "Just one fairy light?"

"No."

"Like… a small one? Subtle twinkle?"

"Fairy lights are a slippery slope. First twinkle, then bunting, then someone's gluing rhinestones to a fire extinguisher."

Sam stepped inside. The floor creaked ominously beneath her shoe. The air was thick with dust and potential. Or possibly asbestos.

"We could actually do this," she said, softly. Almost reverently.

"Do what?" asked Mo, from a safe distance near the door.

"Turn it into a base," Sam said. "Our space. For sessions. Swapping skills. Being chaotic, but like… on purpose."

"A community hub," whispered Rupa, eyes gleaming with biscuit-fuelled vision. "With shelves."

Lee perked up. "Shelves. Yes. We need at least five."

Ronnie held up a small, slightly sticky, probably cursed key. "If you're serious, it's yours. But I swear, if someone starts choreographing a tap dance about compost, I'll sell this place and open a flower shop."

Sam took the key.

It was cold. Old. Slightly bendy. The kind of key you'd expect to unlock a crypt, or Lee's biscuit tin.

And just like that, they had a room.

They stood there for the next hour, not really doing much except believing. Talking in half-sentences. Measuring with shoes. Pointing at cracks like they meant something. Tasha tried to "listen to the energy of the walls" while Mo tried to open the window and nearly lost a thumb.

By the end of the day:

- The dead plant had been given a send-off involving a carrier bag and awkward salutes.

- Rupa found a mug under a chair that said, "World's Best Boss" in Comic Sans and declared it Sam's, because "accidental leadership is still leadership."

- Ronnie brought in bin bags, rubber gloves, and the air of someone quietly regretting all life choices since 1989.

- Lee made a list of required tools, which included a level, a drill, and - obviously - "a packet of biscuits."

Sam stood in the doorway as the light faded outside, holding the key and watching her friends sweep, stack, and repurpose what was basically a glorified shed with delusions of grandeur.

"It's not much," she said.

Mo glanced up, brushing cobwebs from his cardigan. "No. But it's ours."

And for a moment, everything went still. Even the rogue broom in the corner stopped threatening to fall over.

Until it did. Loudly. And with flourish.

Tasha clutched her heart. "The room approves."

Sam smiled.

It was a mess.

It was dusty.

It was almost definitely breaking several health codes.

But it was *theirs*.

And next week?

Next week they were buying a kettle.

Dust, Paint, and Something Taking Shape

They arrived at 9 a.m. on a Saturday with enough energy to power a school fête and the collective DIY knowledge of a soggy instruction manual. Nobody had slept properly. Everyone had brought snacks. And only two of them remembered to bring things actually useful for decorating a room.

Sam bounded in holding a pack of biscuits like a trophy. "I bring gifts!"

"They're digestives," Lee muttered, lugging in a toolbox that clanked ominously.

"Yeah, but the chocolate kind," she grinned. "We're not animals."

Ronnie was already inside, armed with a bin bag, a face like thunder, and a roll of tape that had seen better decades.

"If you break anything," they warned, eyes narrowing as Mo tried to unfold a stepladder backwards, "I'll break you. Tea's in the pot. Mugs are communal. Glitter is punishable by exile. Or worse - a chat with my cousin Glen."

There was a collective shudder. No one had met Glen, but they'd all heard the stories, so his name alone conjured images of unsolicited pyramid schemes and loud opinions about bin day.

The room - formerly known as "the back bit we don't go into" - still looked like it had hosted an awkward exorcism and then tried to cover it up with a doily. The wallpaper had peeled in protest. A chair in the corner looked like it was actively plotting something. And the whole place smelled vaguely of ghostly cheese.

But today, something had changed.

Maybe it was the key Sam now kept in her pocket. Maybe it was the fact no one laughed when she'd called it "ours." Maybe it was the blackboard Mo had already installed without anyone seeing him do it. The man had stealth.

They broke into pairs. Well, "pairs" was a generous term. It was more like strategic chaos with occasional teamwork.

- Rupa and Lee tackled the furniture, creating an impromptu triage system for chairs: Safe, Suspicious, and Possibly Possessed.

- Tasha and Mo took on the fabrics, during which Tasha discovered an old curtain and immediately fashioned it into a cape. "For ambience," she explained, spinning. Mo pretended not to be impressed but adjusted the hem when she wasn't looking.

- Sam painted the back wall a calming shade of blue called Hopeful Mist, which she somehow got in her hair, up her sleeve, and inside her sock. No one asked how. They were too afraid.

"Why does this paint smell like mint?" asked Tasha.

"It's probably the mist," said Sam, wiping her nose on a sleeve she had just painted.

At one point, Rupa opened a dusty box marked *STAFF USE ONLY* and screamed.

"I thought it was a sock!" she cried, wielding a mop like a battleaxe.

"It had knees," muttered Sam, still visibly pale.

"I think it was wearing a hat," Mo added helpfully.

By lunchtime, they were splattered in paint, covered in dust, and weirdly proud. The room wasn't perfect, but it had gone from abandoned broom closet to slightly wonky haven in just a few hours.

The mismatched chairs had been arranged in a lopsided semicircle that Tasha insisted was "feng-chaotic." A tea corner had emerged, complete with kettle, questionable mugs, and a sign from Rupa that read:

Boil with kindness.

Fairy lights twinkled gently above, technically unauthorised but "undetectable if Ronnie doesn't look up."

Mo plugged in the kettle and declared, with the gravitas of a man discovering fire, "We are operational."

They gathered around the centre table - which had one short leg and a sticker on the underside that said *Property of Sue (Do Not Steal)* - and poured tea into mugs with messages like *Keep Calm and Bake Something* and *I Run on Caffeine*.

"It's not fancy," Sam said, looking around at their slightly haphazard creation.

"It's better," Rupa replied, proudly handing out her slightly burnt flapjacks.

"It's alive," whispered Tasha, who had by this point given the room a name:

The Workshop Café.

Lee adjusted a shelf. "It's got heart."

Sam sighed and smiled. The scent of dust, biscuits, and possibility swirled around her. And then, just as she was about to reach for a second flapjack, Ronnie walked in.

They stopped in the doorway. Took it all in. The lights. The paint. The cape. The curtain that was now being used as a tablecloth-slash-stage-backdrop. And then they did something no one expected.

They didn't say a word.

They just walked in, placed their cleaning cloth on the windowsill, and left the door wide open behind them.

Which, by Ronnie standards, was basically a standing ovation and a heartfelt sonnet.

"I think they like it," whispered Mo.

"Or they're too shocked to process emotions," Lee offered.

"Same difference," said Sam, raising her mug in triumph.

They all sat for a while in the warm, slightly musty glow of shared effort and accidental community building.

Outside, the world carried on - dogs barked, buses whooshed, and someone in the next street was having a row with a pigeon. But in here, in this cobbled-together corner of togetherness, something had taken root.

On the front door, they'd tacked up a sign:

The Workshop Café.

Drop In. Join In. No Experience Required.

Below that, in handwriting suspiciously similar to Tasha's:

Tea mandatory. Mistakes welcome. No glitter.

They had a base.

They had a name.

They had each other.

And next week, for the first time, they'd open that slightly sticky door... and see who else might wander in, needing a skill, a cuppa, or just somewhere they wouldn't be judged for wearing a curtain.

Which, as far as Sam was concerned, was the true spirit of community.

From Brew to Boom

Open Door, Open Chaos

The sign on the café door read:

The Workshop Café.

Drop In. Join In. No Experience Required. Tea Mandatory.

Underneath, in glitter pen (which was definitely against policy), someone - absolutely Tasha - had added:

No glitter. By decree of Ronnie.

And below that, in biro:

Maybe a little glitter. Secretly. - Mo

It was opening day. The big launch. The debut performance of what could only be described as a community orchestra made up entirely of triangles, kazoos, and one very optimistic tambourine.

Sam had arrived early. Not to prepare, but to hide in the broom cupboard with a mug of tea and a mild panic. It was her pre-event ritual now, a small private moment of "what are we doing and why do I have so many clipboards?"

Rupa showed up next, carrying a biscuit tin and a strange aura of serene power. Her biscuits were arranged not by type, but by vibe. Digestives for comfort. Custard creams for introverts. Jammy Dodgers for people pretending they didn't need to talk about their feelings.

Tasha swept in, literally, wearing what she called her "welcoming cape" - which had once been a curtain and still carried the faint smell of Dettol. She'd also brought a stack of name badges with glittery borders, which she tried to pass off as "eco-sparkle." Ronnie had already confiscated two.

Mo had set himself up behind a sewing machine like he was guarding a national treasure. He didn't speak much, but his expression said, "Approach me only if thread-related."

Lee, who had somehow already fixed a chair, the toaster, and someone's emotional baggage, was hiding in the corner with a spirit level and a mug labelled *'Mildly Helpful.'*

They hadn't planned anything. At all.

There was no schedule. No formal welcome. No icebreaker activities involving string or marshmallows. Just a few tables, a teetering pile of fabric, some Sharpies, a glue gun, and a sign-up sheet that still only had one entry - a doodle of what appeared to be a motivational potato.

At 10:07 a.m., the door creaked open like it knew this was going to be weird.

A man poked his head in. Late thirties. Mildly windswept. "Is this the coffee tasting event?"

Sam blinked. "Er... not officially?"

"Cool," he said, stepping inside. "Got time to kill."

At 10:22, a woman wandered in, bleary-eyed, holding her coat like it had personally betrayed her. She said nothing, made a cup of tea, and sat down as though she'd always lived there.

By 11:00 a.m., the room was... alive.

Not packed. Not buzzing. But gently, wonderfully busy - like a teabag steeping in hot water, growing stronger by the minute.

Sam, unsure of where to be, tried to be everywhere. She drifted with the energy of someone doing an interpretive dance titled *"I Am Organised, I Swear."* Her main job appeared to be refilling the biscuit plate every five minutes and pretending the clipboard she was holding meant something.

At 11:22, everything changed.

She leaned against a chair. Sighed. Then tried to stand up - only to realise she couldn't.

Her sleeve was stuck.

To the chair.

Sam froze, then glanced down and saw, with the quiet despair of a woman who had already made several bad decisions that week, the telltale shimmer of superglue.

She whispered, "Help."

Lee strolled over, looked at the situation, and said calmly, "Of course you've glued yourself to a chair."

"In fairness," Sam whispered back, "technically it's my sleeve that's glued."

Lee, who had clearly seen worse, passed her a tiny flathead tool. "I'll get the chair. You distract everyone."

"How?"

"Do what you usually do. Talk."

Sam nodded. Then stood - bringing the chair with her.

There was a squeak. A silence. A collective inhale.

Then Tasha clapped. "Performance art! I love it."

Sam gave a shaky bow. The chair bowed too. A duet.

Eventually, Mo performed a delicate rescue using tweezers, a hairdryer, and the kind of precision found in bomb disposal. Lee sanded down the glue stain, Rupa offered a sympathy custard cream, and Tasha began brainstorming a new workshop idea titled *'Crafting with Chaos: When Furniture Becomes You.'*

By midday, things were properly rolling.

Someone was teaching someone else how to sew on a button. Someone else was explaining council tax. A group of three were trying to learn origami from a very confusing YouTube tutorial on mute. And somehow, without anyone remembering who started it, a communal pot of coffee had appeared and was quietly bubbling on a hot plate by the window.

"I think this counts as a success," Rupa whispered, her voice hushed as though scared the coffee might hear and disappear.

Sam nodded, watching a woman she didn't know teach a boy how to thread a sewing machine.

"We did that," she murmured.

"Well," Mo said, appearing beside her, "we opened a door."

"They came in."

"That's how it starts."

They stood for a moment in the hum of it all.

There was laughter. The scribble of pens. The occasional frustrated noise of someone battling a tangled ball of wool. On one table, someone had written *"Things I Might Be Good At"* on the back of a napkin and was slowly adding to it, one biscuit-fuelled revelation at a time.

Lee fixed another wobbly chair. Tasha was leading a trust exercise that involved passing a teacup using only elbows. Ronnie, from the counter, pretended not to care - but left out a fresh plate of shortbread and a sign that said, *"Use a coaster or I cry."*

Sam leaned against the counter, being careful of her sleeve, which was still slightly sticky.

It wasn't polished.

It wasn't perfect.

But it was open.

The Teen, the Thread, and the Hoodie Rescue

He didn't say much when he came in.

Just nodded once at the sign, once at the biscuits, and held up a hoodie like a peace offering.

It was grey, oversized, and torn down the side. Not fashionably ripped - forgot-to-dodge-a-gatepost ripped. The sleeve hung like it had given up on life entirely.

Sam spotted him first. "Hey! Need help?"

He gave the smallest shrug.

"Mo's your guy," she said, gently steering him towards the sewing table. "He's basically the Sewing Whisperer. Also drinks tea like it's a life strategy."

Mo looked up, blinked once, and nodded. "Sit."

The boy sat. Still hadn't said a word.

Mo examined the hoodie, ran a thumb gently along the frayed edge like a doctor checking for a pulse.

"Stitch or patch?"

The boy shrugged again, then pointed to a scrap of denim in the fabric box.

"Patch it is."

They worked in silence - Mo threading the needle like he was performing delicate surgery, the boy watching, arms folded, expression unreadable. Every now and then, Mo held up the hoodie, showed him what he was doing. The boy nodded. They carried on.

Sam tried not to hover.

Rupa passed them biscuits.

Tasha wandered over, took one look, and whispered, "This is so going in the montage."

Twenty-five minutes later, the patch was in place. Not flashy. Not perfect. But neat. Solid. Held together with strong stitches and the kind of care you couldn't fake.

Mo handed it back. The boy held it like it was something new - not just mended, but different.

"Thanks," he said quietly.

Then he smiled.

Not a big smile. Not one of Tasha's theatrical grins or Sam's slightly chaotic *everything's fine* smiles.

Just a small, lopsided, genuine one.

The boy stood up, put the hoodie back on, and looked... taller.

Not physically. Just... more him.

He held out his hand to Mo, "Name's Ash. Thank you."

Tasha clapped once. "Right. Group power pose!"

Mo took his hand. "Welcome."

Everyone groaned.

"Come on," she insisted, striking a heroic stance. "Hands on hips. Chins up. It's SCIENCE. Builds confidence!"

Sam joined in - partly for moral support, partly to stretch out a glue-stiffened shoulder.

Rupa did it while still holding a tea towel.

Mo refused, but allowed one eyebrow to twitch in reluctant solidarity.

Even the boy - eventually - joined in.

He stood with them, awkwardly heroic, hoodie patched and posture proud.

Ronnie watched from the counter, shook their head, and muttered, "Absolute weirdos." But they smiled.

Later, as they all packed up, Sam nudged Mo.

"That was good, what you did."

"I stitched a sleeve."

"You stitched a moment."

Mo rolled his eyes, but his ears went slightly pink.

"You changed his whole vibe," Sam added. "He walked in slouching. He left... upright."

"Could've been the biscuits."

"Could've been the care."

Mo didn't reply. But he packed the sewing kit a little more gently.

Sam watched him for a second, then wrote something on the blackboard for tomorrow's drop-in:

Fix what you can. Stitch what matters. Tea at 10.

Brenda Brings Biscuits

They heard her before they saw her.

"Is this the thing with the kettle and the what-do-you-call-it? The fixing, the teaching, the mucking in?"

Sam looked up from where she was arranging. "That sounds... like us, yes."

The door swung open in the most theatrical way and in marched a woman of purpose, presence, and pastel outerwear. Her coat was the colour of blind optimism in cardigan form. Her shoes meant business. And under one arm, she clutched a large, suspiciously dented tin like it contained either freshly baked goods or the secrets to national security.

"I've brought biscuits," she announced, without waiting for an introduction. "And a phone that's smarter than me. I want help with one and praise for the other."

She dropped the tin on the table with a thud that echoed off the fairy-lit walls like a declaration of war.

"Shortbread," she said. "Homemade. Unless I hate you, in which case you can have the broken ones."

Several people moved very quickly to be liked.

Brenda - and she would later insist it was "Brenda. Not Bren. Not B. Not love. I am not your nan or your cat."

Brenda was in her seventies. She wore pearls with trainers, sarcasm like it was perfume, and the kind of expression that said she'd once shouted at a politician and made them apologise in writing.

Lee offered her a mug of tea.

She took it, sniffed it, sipped it, and gave a solemn nod. "Acceptable."

Mo asked if she liked sewing.

"I prefer biscuits," she replied. "They don't answer back."

Tasha leaned in. "That's fair."

Then came the phone. She pulled it from her handbag like it was going to explode.

"This thing keeps yelling at me. Notifications, updates, vibrations. There's a woman called Siri who keeps offering to do things I didn't ask for. I tried to tell her off, but she just played Bon Jovi."

Rupa, brave and soft in equal measure, patted the seat beside her. "Let's have a look."

Brenda carefully handed the phone over, sure Siri might protest at any moment.

The next forty minutes were what scientists might call a "technological breakthrough

Rupa taught her how to:

- Check messages without accidentally ordering nine electric kettles.
  Silence Siri – for good.

- Update her apps without deleting the entire internet.

- Block a man named "Tony Maybe," who had been sending increasingly shirtless photos and once invited her to "a private bowls strategy meeting."

"Not today, Tony," Brenda muttered, jabbing the delete button. "Your chest is not the content I came for."

From a distance, Sam watched the entire exchange unfold with the awe of someone witnessing a very polite exorcism. She sipped her tea, fell slightly in love, and whispered to Mo, "We've just found our queen."

By the time the tea had cooled to room temperature and the shortbread had been reduced to crumbs and legend, Brenda had:

- Subscribed to a YouTube channel called Purl & Panic ("They knit while arguing. It's gripping.")

- Sent her first emoji ("The one with the big eyes - very expressive, like a shocked owl.")

- Agreed to run a drop-in session next week. "But only if people promise not to talk through it."

Before she left, she turned to Lee, who had fixed a shelf and said precisely three words all morning.

161

"You're the quiet one."

He nodded.

"You're a marvel."

He blinked. "I… thank you."

Then she turned to Rupa and held her gaze like a psychic peering into her soul.

"And you, my love," she said, "are worth more than any of these biscuits. And that's saying something."

Rupa teared up. Not full sobbing - more like an emotional misting.

"I've got banana muffins too," she whispered, shoving a Tupperware into Brenda's hands like an offering to a biscuit deity.

Sam opened the door with a grin. Brenda paused in the doorway, sunlight catching the sparkle of defiance in her eyes.

"I'll be back," she said, like she was leaving a threat or a prophecy. "You've made something good here. Don't mess it up."

"Wouldn't dare," Sam replied, hand over heart.

Brenda gave a regal nod, adjusted her bag, and marched off into the afternoon with her tin, her phone, and her freshly updated sense of digital dominance.

The silence she left behind was filled, quite naturally, by Sam.

162

"We need a plaque."

Mo looked up. "For the wall?"

"For her."

Tasha clapped her hands. "Yes! **Brenda: Bringer of Biscuits. Destroyer of Tony**. We could even put it above the kettle."

Rupa sniffled.

Sam smiled.

Tasha wrote **'Baked by Brenda'** on a Post-It and stuck it to the biscuit tin - lovingly, like a badge of honour.

And Mo, who hadn't smiled all day, glanced at the empty shortbread plate and murmured, "Next time, we request Viennese whirls."

Café Corners and Small Miracles

It happened entirely by accident.

Or, more accurately - because Ronnie forgot to shut the door.

Not the front one. That had its usual assortment of creaks and a bell that sounded like an aggressive wind chime.

No, it was *the* door. The one at the back. The one to The Workshop Café's newly painted, slightly uneven, possibly haunted home base.

The door that, until now, had been treated with the sacred reverence of museum exhibits and posh biscuits.

Ronnie had left it open. Just a crack. Enough for steam to curl out like gossip, and for curiosity to slip in behind someone looking for the loo.

And then... people wandered in.

The first was a man in his late sixties wearing a high-vis jacket and a face that hadn't smiled since dial-up internet. He poked his head around the corner, squinted, and asked, "Is this the council office?"

Sam, mid-biscuit arrangement (cranberry digestives forming a sacred pentagon of welcome), looked up. "Nope. But we do have tea."

He hovered. She offered a ginger nut. He sat down for ten minutes. Left with directions to the town hall, basic instructions on how to use email, and a lentil recipe from Rupa that ended with, "or just add cheese and hope for the best."

The second was a mum in a puffa coat that had seen better days with a small child in tow who never made eye contact.

"We're just looking for somewhere warm," she said, eyes tired.

"You found it," said Tasha, swooping in with cushions, crayons, and the kind of smile that made you feel like a long-lost relative.

Masha, the mum in the puffa jacket, stayed for tea. The child sat next to her almost glued to her sleeve, and silently scribbled in her notebook, occasionally daydreaming. Rupa had a chat with her about cooking on a budget that would make a potato cry, slipping in her mum's trick about stretching curry with chickpeas instead of meat.

At the next table, a small group were swapping vocabulary - English words for the café regulars, Gujarati and Polish words going back the other way, everyone laughing at the mispronunciations.

Often the words were about food – the great connector – people from different sides of the globe united in a common interest.

By 11:00, the back room had shifted from "mildly organised chaos" to "community chaos with extra people."

No one knew what was happening.

But it was... happening.

People popped their heads in, paused like they'd walked into a new world via the broom cupboard, and just... stayed.

Some stayed for the chat.

Some stayed for the tea.

Some stayed for the chance to sit somewhere they weren't expected to buy a latte or explain their life story.

Mo, cool as ever, taught a woman how to sew a hem using only a paperclip, a kind word, and ancient sewing wisdom that might've involved whispering to the fabric.

Tasha led an impromptu "Confidence Through Coat-Hanger Posture" session, which involved shouting things like "YOU ARE THE WARDROBE OF YOUR OWN DESTINY!" while people tried not to spill tea.

Lee silently fixed the café's coat rack, then alphabetised the teabags.

When asked why, he just said, "It needed doing," and refused to elaborate.

At one point, Sam spotted a teenage girl showing an older man how to use a QR code.

"What does it do?" he asked.

The girl shrugged. "Does it matter? It works."

Tasha looked like someone had just written her a sonnet.

"That," she whispered, "was theatre."

Ronnie walked past with a tea towel and muttered, "That was free Wi-Fi, love." But the reason people were coming didn't matter, they were turning up anyway.

Then there was Brenda.

She wasn't supposed to be there.

She popped in to "drop off a few biscuits" and explicitly stated, "I am NOT staying."

Within eight minutes she had:

- Rearranged the mug shelf.

- Started a debate on the best type of budgeting biscuit (shortbread won, digestive staged a protest).

She stayed for an hour and left with a tote bag, two phone numbers, and a new catchphrase:

"Don't let the finances bite - bite back."

By midday, the whole café felt like it had expanded by at least ten square metres.

People were pouring tea for strangers.

Someone wiped down a table and ended up learning how to fold origami birds out of napkins.

Ash helped Mo fix a crochet blanket one of the old ladies had brought in.

A woman started crying halfway through sorting fabric. No one asked why. They just handed her a biscuit and made space.

Someone even asked if they could just sit quietly for a bit.

The group nodded so seriously it was like they'd been trained in Silent Sitting Consent.

Sam, mid-cup-of-tea and covered in a suspicious patch of glue (again), leaned against the doorframe and just... took it all in.

She didn't say anything for a while.

She just watched.

Mo threading a needle.

Tasha explaining "personal flair" to a boy using feathers.

Lee adjusting the fairy lights so they didn't resemble a festive fire hazard.

Brenda offering unsolicited life advice with the intensity of a woman who once wrote to *Watchdog* and won.

Finally, Sam turned to Rupa and said, quietly, "This is something, right?"

Rupa, holding a chipped mug and a heart full of new names, nodded.

"This is everything."

Ronnie passed by with a tray of clean mugs.

They looked at the room - really looked.

Then said, "Don't get soppy. You'll flood the floor."

But they left the tray, and they left the door open.

Which, from Ronnie, was basically permission and affection.

By the end of the day, three people signed up to run sessions - including "Slow Cooking for the Impatient" and "How Not to Get Scammed by That Guy on Facebook Again."

Someone made a new sign:

The Workshop Café.

Come In. Join In. Tea Mandatory.

Sam sat on a slightly uneven chair, smiling at the community they hadn't quite meant to build - at least not like this.

It wasn't what she'd imagined.

It wasn't neat, or planned, or properly laminated.

But it was open.

And open was enough.

The Coat Rack of Community

Mo didn't announce he was building a coat rack.

There was no group vote. No sub-committee. No laminated sign-up sheet headed **'RACK PLANNING AGENDA.'**

He just... turned up one Tuesday morning with a plank of wood under one arm and a quiet sense of purpose that made people get out of his way without quite knowing why.

Sam spotted him in the back room, mid-measure, eyes narrowed like a laser level had personally offended him.

He was measuring the wall with the sort of concentration of a nuclear physicist.

"You okay?" Sam asked, holding a mug of tea and a custard cream like a comfort offering.

Mo nodded without looking up. "Mm-hmm."

"What's that?" she tried again, because the wall was now covered in chalk lines and something that looked suspiciously like a diagram titled 'Load-Bearing Support Hooks.'

"Coat rack," he said simply.

"Oh. Nice." She paused. "Why?"

"Thought people might want somewhere to leave things."

Sam blinked. "You mean like… emotionally, or…"

"Scarves. Hats. Gloves… in case somebody needs them."

"Ah. Less metaphorical."

He worked quietly, methodically, and with the kind of calm that suggested he had absolutely built things before - possibly barns or bridges.

By the time Sam had finished her tea (and eaten the biscuit purely for health reasons), Mo had sanded the plank, fitted six hooks, and labelled it with a small hand-lettered sign:

Hang here. Warm someone up.

They mounted it by the door, slightly crooked but full of charm - like everything else in the place.

By lunchtime, people were already noticing.

It wasn't announced.

There was no trumpet fanfare, no interpretive dance from Tasha (though she did suggest one).

But still… they came.

The first offering was a red woollen scarf.

Frayed at the ends. Folded over a hook with quiet dignity. No tag. No note. Just… there.

A few hours later, a pair of mittens joined - small, navy blue, slightly pilled, clearly loved.

Then a hat.

Then two.

Then a beige bobble hat that Mo regarded with suspicion until it won him over by matching the hooks.

And then came the note.

Pinned just above the middle hook, in neat handwriting that definitely wasn't Mo's (he later denied this five times and blushed once):

'Take one if you're cold.'

And underneath it, in totally different handwriting (and suspiciously glittery pen):

'Leave one if you can.'

Sam stared at it for a long moment, feeling something fuzzy bloom in her chest.

"Did you write this?" she asked Mo, who was dusting nearby like a butler who moonlighted as a carpenter.

He shook his head. "Not me."

"Lee?"

Lee looked up from rearranging the tea station into what could only be described as a hot beverage sculpture. "I... don't own glitter."

"Tasha?"

She gasped. "I was rehearsing my *Coat Monologue*! I missed the whole emotional beat!"

Even Ronnie denied involvement - though they did mutter, "I don't own glitter pens, I own dignity," while hiding something suspiciously sparkly in their apron.

"Well," Sam said, standing back with her hands on her hips, "I love it. It's warm. In every way."

Mo poured a cup of tea and slipped outside.

Sam followed with her eyes through the café window and saw him hand it quietly to the same man who'd been sheltering near the bins the week before.

No fuss. No words. Just a cup of warmth passed from one pair of hands to another.

By mid-afternoon, Sam noticed the man again - this time stepping inside, moving carefully as if he wasn't sure he belonged, and leaving with a scarf draped over his shoulders.

By Thursday, the coat rack was officially 'A Thing'.

Not an initiative. Not a project. Just... a thing people did.

Scarves came and went.

Hats rotated in and out like polite guests at a tea party.

Masha dropped by and her little girl left with earmuffs that made her look like a tiny panda.

A teenager came in one day soaked to the bone, sleeves dripping, face pink with embarrassment. He left twenty minutes later wearing a dry hoodie someone had left behind and the world's most careful smile.

One man tried to donate ski trousers the size of a yurt. Mo quietly steered him toward the donation bin outside with a gentle pat and a whispered, "Let's not frighten the locals."

By Friday, someone had crocheted a handful of tiny hearts and tied them to each hook.

Tasha cried actual tears, declared it "performance kindness with no stage fright," and tried to hug everyone before getting tangled in a scarf chain.

Sam stood by it often. Just watched.

Not because it was grand.

But because it wasn't.

There were no forms. No logins. No performance metrics.

Just people giving what they could. Taking what they needed.

Like a quiet barter system of love and wool.

"Someone left a hat with ear flaps," Rupa whispered one day. "I nearly cried. It was lined."

"It's a revolution," Sam said. "One pom-pom at a time."

Mo, meanwhile, took to dusting the rack every morning like it was the crown jewels.
Lee made a tiny blackboard to track the "in and out" hat count.

Brenda offered to make hat tags that said **'Warm me. Don't wash me on high.'**

And Sam… well, Sam laminated.

Of course she did.

She made a sign and tacked it gently to the side of the rack:

'Everything here has been left with love.

Take what you need. Leave what you can.

No questions. No thanks needed.

(Except maybe to Mo.)'

Ronnie walked past it on Saturday, arms full of mugs, glanced at the whole setup and sniffed.

"If someone hangs tinsel on that thing," they muttered, "I'm setting it on fire."

Sam grinned. "Noted."

They hung fairy lights instead.

Soft. Twinkly. Just enough glow to say "you're welcome" without being smug about it.

By the end of the month, the coat rack had a name.

Not official. Just whispered. Shared.

'Cosy Corner.'

No one admitted to naming it.

But every time someone walked in, wet and weary, and left warmer and straighter backed... well, no one needed to say it.

Mo just nodded.

Sam refilled the tea.

Tasha's Big Day

It happened by accident.

As most brilliant things in the café did.

Tasha claimed she was chilled. Calm. Unflappable. "Zen with jazz hands," she'd said.

But Sam had seen the truth.

There were signs. Dramatic signs. Literal signs.

The extra scarves. The suspiciously large tote bag that jingled ominously. The way she muttered, "Circle of Life" under her breath while rearranging cardboard crowns in a perfect rainbow of royal expression.

Today was Mini Improv Magic - her first official children's session.

Ronnie had renamed it, with much less enthusiasm:

'Loud Children in My Café, Send Help.'

They'd set up early, mainly so Tasha could create her 'theatrical environment' and Mo could plug things in without panic.

The setup was... ambitious.

A half-circle of tiny chairs. A squishy rug borrowed from the storeroom. Puppets crafted from socks, spatulas, a surprising number of spoons, and one suspiciously hairy thing no one wanted to touch.

Mo brought his Bluetooth speaker and tested it with a single, dramatic "DUN DUN DUUUUN!" sound effect that made a toddler cry and Lee drop a teacup.

Lee also made a sign.

It said:

'ROAR ZONE.'

He immediately regretted it.

By 10:15, the back room was full. Packed, actually.

Children buzzed around like hyper bees in trainers, ranging in age from "four and covered in stickers" to "ten and legally allergic to sitting still."

Parents hovered at the edges like nervous festival security.

One grandad came in looking for a quiet cuppa and ended up adopting a googly-eyed spoon named Kevin.

Tasha stood front and centre, a vision of floaty layers and optimistic charm.

She clapped her hands. "Welcome, my drama dynamos! Today, you can be anything - dragons, detectives, planets, or potatoes with feelings!"

A tiny boy leapt to his feet, flailing wildly. "I'm a rainbow who does karate!"

"Excellent," said Tasha, with a bow. "Front row. You're now Head of Glitter Security."

And from there, all structure disintegrated in the most glorious, biscuit-fuelled way imaginable.

They roared like dinosaurs.

They danced like wind-up jellyfish.

They improvised an entire scene where a pirate and a unicorn opened a sandwich shop on the moon. Sam played the world's grumpiest customer. Rupa was the unimpressed health inspector. Mo provided live sound effects using a colander, a teaspoon, and a deeply unsettling squelch app.

Kevin the Spoon kept appearing in increasingly chaotic cameos, once declaring a tax audit mid-scene.

Masha and her daughter were there. She was a shy girl in a yellow jumper standing quietly at the edge, twisting her sleeve and watching from behind a chair.

Tasha clocked her immediately.

She knelt beside her with the grace of someone who understood that not all spotlights are welcome.

"Want to join?" she asked gently.

The girl shook her head, clutching her tatty frog toy like it was a legal requirement.

"That's okay," Tasha whispered. "You can help me. I need someone to guard the crown jewels. And possibly stop Kevin the Spoon from starting another fire."

The girl shook her head more firmly and sat down to draw in her book.

Masha leaned into Sam. "Don't worry she doesn't like to join in."

Sam didn't know what to say, she just smiled.

By the end of the session, the children clapped for each other like they'd just completed *Hamilton* and earned a knighthood.

"Thank you!" Tasha beamed. "You were all magnificent! Now go home and tell someone you're secretly a dragon!"

The kids filed out, buzzing like fizzy drinks in human form.

One left behind a sock puppet with only one eye.

Tasha placed it gently on a shelf.

Sam passed her a mug of tea. "That was... honestly... magic."

Tasha sniffled. "It's just... the dust."

"Glitter dust?"

"Shut up."

Ronnie passed by with a tray of clean mugs, paused, surveyed the remains of the day - crumpled puppets, trail of stickers, three jammy dodgers on the ceiling - and sighed.

"If you're planning to do this every week," they said, "I'm raising the biscuit budget."

"Wait," said Tasha, eyes wide. "Are you saying we're allowed?"

Ronnie gave her 'The Look' - part warning, part affection, part *'you bring glitter near the till and I'll end you.'*

"Only if Kevin the Spoon retires," they said flatly. "He's a menace."

"I can't control him," Tasha said solemnly. "He's freelance."

Everyone laughed.

Sam looked around - the rumpled rug, the paper crowns, the sock puppets now slumped like actors post-show. But all she could think of was Masha's little girl – and she didn't even know her name.

She took a long sip of tea and breathed it all in.

Tasha didn't need a stage.

She'd built one.

Out of spoon puppets, silly voices, and a belief that children are brilliant when you give them space and snacks.

As the others tidied up, Lee carefully removed a glitter sticker from his elbow and muttered, "Why is this shaped like a flamingo?"

"It's avant-garde," Tasha grinned.

Sam picked up Kevin and held him at eye level. "Be honest - are you cursed?" Kevin said nothing.

But somehow... judged her.

Tasha reached out and plucked him gently from Sam's hand. "Kevin's taking a break," she said. "Union rules."

They packed up. Folded chairs. Wiped jam. Retrieved three puppets from inside a potted plant.

Mo adjusted the fairy lights. Rupa boxed the surviving biscuits. Sam scribbled on the blackboard:

Next Session:

Mini Improv Magic – Part 2

Bring your own sock. Or spoon. Or crown.

As the lights dimmed, the back room of Ronnie's café didn't feel like a café at all. It felt like a stage, a playground, a space where the shyest kid could become a fearless ruler of googly-eyed puppets and root vegetables.

And just before she left, Tasha glanced over her shoulder at the puppet on the shelf and whispered, "Your time will come, one-eyed Steve."

The Council Nearly Get Involved

It began - as so many terrifying things do - with a clipboard and a tie.

Which, in most normal spaces, might suggest "professionalism."

But in a café that smells faintly of glue sticks, coffee, and ambition, it meant only one thing:

Panic.

At exactly 10:32 a.m. on a perfectly innocent Thursday, a man in smart shoes and a coat that screamed "civic responsibility" stepped through the café doors.

Sam, mid-bite of a biscuit, froze like she'd been caught eating tax returns.

Mo paused mid-stitch, needle in hand, as if waiting for the word "confiscated."

Tasha dropped her glitter pen, eyes wide. "Oh no," she whispered. "Is this about the fairy lights? I knew they'd find out."

Rupa stood up so fast she knocked over a mug, shouted "SORRY" before it even hit the floor, and clutched her apron like it was a flotation device.

Lee - somehow already holding a cloth - sighed and began mopping.

The man blinked. He looked mildly alarmed but... undeterred. Like someone who once attended a parish council meeting and survived.

"Hello," he said, in the carefully neutral tone of someone who's walked into both a toddler group and a minor uprising and isn't yet sure which this is.

"I'm from the council."

You could hear the collective gulp.

"Oh no," said Sam, which she hadn't meant to say out loud.

"I was told about this group - The Workshop Café?" He checked his clipboard like it might suddenly shout 'RUN!' "We just wanted to... pop in. Get a feel for things. No pressure."

Sam stepped forward. She wasn't sure if she should shake his hand or offer him a loyalty card.

"Hi! Yes! Welcome! We're very... casual."

"We do help," Rupa added quickly. "There's tea. And fixing. Sometimes cake, but that's unpredictable."

"It's not a cult," Mo said.

"Definitely not a cult," Tasha echoed, eyes darting. "Unless someone's bringing robes. Are you bringing robes?"

The man's face went blank, trying to take it all in.

"No robes. Just… curiosity. And, uh, maybe a few questions about insurance?"

That did it.

Chaos.

Sam's brain imploded.

"Do we have insurance?" she hissed to Rupa.

"Was someone supposed to get insurance?" Rupa hissed back, suddenly furious with Past Rupa for being so casual with paperwork.

"Do biscuits count as a safety measure?" Tasha asked.

"Only if they're chocolate-coated," Lee muttered, somehow still mopping.

The man took a hesitant step forward. "Honestly, I just want to see what you do. A colleague's mum came last week - said it changed her week."

At that moment, Brenda arrived - as she always did - like a sitcom entrance with impeccable timing.

A tin of shortbread under one arm, her pearls swinging as she walked.

"Tea?" she said brightly, handing him a mug with the effortless menace of a mafia don offering espresso.

"Budgeting session starts in ten," she added, slamming her folder down on the table like she was about to audit his soul. "But we can fast-track you if you're scared of percentages."

The man sat down. He didn't so much choose the chair as submit to it.

Sam watched, still trying to work out if they were in trouble or accidentally shortlisted for a King's Award.

"You know," said Brenda, opening her laminated attack plan, "it's shocking how many people don't know what they're spending on utilities."

"I - well - my gas bill - " the man began.

"No excuses," Brenda said, handing him a pen like a summons. "Write."

And he did.

He dutifully filled in Brenda's handy budget worksheet.

Then he listened to Rupa's lentil recipe and wrote it down under "Essentials."

He nodded earnestly as Mo, and his new sidekick Ash, explained thread tension and the importance of having at least two types of buttons.

Tasha slid him a sparkly notebook that read "Budget Like a Badass." No one stopped her.

He even smiled.

An actual, possibly genuine, possibly enchanted smile.

"I'll... report back," he said eventually, clutching his shortbread and spreadsheet like newly discovered treasure.

Sam walked him to the door, still half-expecting a surprise inspection or a fine for 'excessive community cohesion.'

But before he left, he turned to her.

"You know," he said softly, "this is what people mean when they talk about community. It's messy. It's brilliant. And somehow, you're holding it all together with tea and tape."

Sam blinked.

Then grinned. "Don't forget glitter glue."

He nodded, solemnly, like she'd quoted policy.

And then he was gone.

The door clicked shut. Silence fell.

For three seconds.

Then the group exhaled.

"So…" said Mo, carefully replacing his stitch marker.

"…we weren't raided?" said Tasha.

"Not today," Rupa said. "Though I did nearly confess to tax fraud when he asked my name."

Lee wiped the last of the tea from the floor. "I think he liked us."

"I think he's traumatised," said Brenda. "In a good way."

Ronnie emerged from the kitchen, arms folded, eyebrow raised.

"Did he ask about the fairy lights?" they said.

"No," said Tasha.

"Then don't tell him."

Sam sat down, heartbeat slowly returning to pre-bureaucratic levels.

"We weren't shut down," she said.

"We were noticed," said Mo.

"And possibly insured," added Rupa.

Tasha raised a biscuit. "To progress!"

Lee raised his mop. "To minimum safety compliance!"

Sam looked around - at the notes on the blackboard, the teacups, the frayed cushions, and the newly added page in the Welcome Folder titled "If The Council Visit, Smile and Offer Brenda."

She took a deep breath and said it again, just to hear how it sounded.

"We're being noticed."

Brenda nodded. "We're official."

Ronnie muttered, "You're all ridiculous."

.

Something's Happening Here

There was a moment - brief, almost missable - when Sam thought Ronnie had lost it.

It was just after morning prep, mid-coffee rush.

Ronnie appeared at the front, a small wooden A-frame clutched in one hand and their usual expression of "don't test me before tea" on full display.

They dumped it on the counter with all the ceremony of a disgruntled librarian returning a late book.

"Found this," they grunted.

Sam squinted at it. "Is that... a sign?"

"It's a blackboard. Behind the expired Earl Grey and something marked Emergency Trifle Kit. You want it or not?"

Sam tilted her head. "Are we being allowed signage?"

"Call it a trial. One rude doodle and I'm setting it on fire."

"That seems fair."

They propped it up outside the café, slightly wobbly on the uneven pavement, like it was auditioning for a job as an optimistic sandwich board.

Rupa got first go with the chalk.

Her handwriting was a thing of gentle loops and domestic power. She scrawled:

Today at The Workshop Café

10 a.m. – Sew & Chat

11:30 – Drama with Tasha (bring a scarf, not trauma)

1 p.m. – Budgeting with Brenda (tea mandatory)

Then someone (suspected: Tasha, confirmed: Tasha) added in a loopy scrawl at the bottom:

Tea and biscuits at two. Judgement absent.

By 9:47 a.m., people were stopping to read it.

By 10:03, someone asked, "What's the Workshop Café?"

Sam paused. "That's us."

"Oh. Nice."

By midweek, the place had transformed again - not physically, but spiritually.

Sam wandered in one afternoon to find a woman she'd never met, sitting at a table, sipping tea and casually crocheting something that looked suspiciously like a llama in sunglasses.

The woman looked up, smiled, and said: "This is the place, isn't it?"

Sam blinked. "Which place?"

"The one where you can just… be."

Sam opened her mouth to reply, then closed it again.

Then nodded. "Yeah. I think it is."

That day, they made:

- A new sign-in sheet titled Join the Mayhem (optional).

- A donation tin rebranded as The Biscuits & Hope Fund.

- An actual rota. With names. And days. And assigned tasks. Mo stared at it like it was holy scripture, then quietly cried into his tea. No one said anything. Rupa handed him a muffin.

Later that night, when the café emptied out and the tables were wiped down (sort of), Sam and Rupa stood in the doorway, mugs in hand, gazing up at the fairy lights.

They were strung between mismatched nails and suspiciously improvised hooks, gently swaying, slightly uneven, and glorious.

"This all started with biscuits," Sam murmured.

Rupa nodded. "And a spreadsheet."

"And a hoodie."

"And a suspiciously charismatic banana."

Sam chuckled. "We didn't plan any of this."

Rupa shrugged. "We planned tea. The rest just... followed."

Ronnie passed by with a tray of leftover muffins. They didn't stop, but they muttered as they went, "Don't get sentimental. You'll attract feelings."

But - and this was key - they didn't lock the door.

And in Ronnie terms? That was the equivalent of a full-blown group hug.

By the time they closed up for the night, the blackboard stood proud out front, still slightly wobbly, but now sporting an extra message:

Welcome to The Workshop Café

Come in for tea. Stay for the weird.

(Mostly the good kind.)

Sam looked at it, hand on the doorframe, heart full of something too big to name.

Not pride, exactly. Not relief.

Something softer. Stranger.

Like belonging with frayed edges.

"Something's happening here," she whispered.

Mo walked past, adjusting a wobbly hook, and said, deadpan, "It already has."

They left the lights on that night. Just for a while. Just because they could.

Because sometimes, a blackboard isn't just a blackboard.

It's a flag.

A signal.

The Ripple Effect

Unexpected Entrepreneurs

It was the hoodie that did it.

Not just any hoodie. *The* hoodie.

Mo's hoodie.

Or rather, Ash's hoodie - once duct-taped at the seams, with a zip that gave up sometime in 2019 and a cuff that had definitely seen a run-in with a Bunsen burner.

Mo had fixed it weeks ago. Quietly. Carefully. The way Mo did everything. One needle. One thread. One stitch closer to something whole.

The teenager had come in shy. Didn't talk much. Always arrived early, always left with a biscuit in his pocket, and sat in that same seat by the back wall like it was his invisibility cloak.

But now?

Now he had an Etsy shop.

Sam blinked as he walked in one Saturday - same boy, same grin - but the hoodie?

It had logos.

Tiny, stitched-on patches. Handmade. Jagged but proud. One on the sleeve said, 'Custom Chaos.' Another on the back, scrawled in thread like a stitched mic drop:

Stitch Happens.

Sam choked on her tea.

"You've got a brand?"

Ash grinned. "Been customising stuff. Started with my own. Then some mates asked. Then someone asked if I'd do it for cash, so... yeah. I set up a shop on Etsy."

Mo wandered over just in time for Sam to half-hug, half-tackle him.

"Did we do this?" she stage-whispered.

Mo blinked. "I'm not crying. It's the lint."

Ash pulled a small business card from his bag – rough-edged but bold. It read:

Learned at The Workshop Café.

"Put you guys on my bio too," he said, like it was the most normal thing in the world.

"You put us... on your bio?"

"Yeah. I figured, I didn't learn this at school. Or online. I learned it here. From you lot."

Sam held the card like it was sacred.

Then promptly stuck it in her notebook using a bit of tape and what might've been icing sugar.

But it wasn't just Ash.

Lately, things had been... spreading.

Not in a grand, billboard-advertisement, ticker-tape-parade kind of way.

In a quiet, lentil-scented, "I just helped someone and now I feel weirdly brilliant" sort of way.

Pauline - Brenda's mate, who used to visibly tremble in the presence of Microsoft Excel - was now helping out in a charity office two mornings a week. Turned up last Thursday with a handbag that could grace a catwalk and a glow like someone who finally understood the difference between direct debits and standing orders.

"Can't believe I'm saying this," she told Lee, holding a budgeting form like it was a winning lottery ticket, "but spreadsheets are kind of... thrilling."

Lee blinked. "Are you okay?"

"No," she beamed. "I'm competent."

Tasha made the entire group do a victory pose.

Mo joined in. Reluctantly. While holding a teacake.

Even Rupa - practical, unflappable, emotional support chef of the group - was starting to find her recipes out there in the world.

She walked into the local church hall for a bring-and-share lunch and found her 'Lentils That Hug Back' stew being served under a sign that read **'as featured in The Workshop Café.'**

Sam nearly fainted with joy.

Rupa just blinked. "They didn't even credit me."

"You're underground famous," said Tasha. "Like Banksy. But with turmeric."

And the best part?

None of it was planned.

No logo. No website. No over-thought business model. Just human beings, doing human things. Helping each other. Learning without realising. Growing sideways, diagonally - and occasionally, accidentally - into their best selves.

It was chaos.

It was glorious.

It was theirs.

Sam stood near the coat rack one Thursday, watching Ash - hoodie champion, introvert extraordinaire - teach a girl how to reinforce the straps on her rucksack using nothing but dental floss and raw determination.

Across the room, someone was showing Pauline how to send a calendar invite.

Someone else was laughing with Rupa about lentil textures.

Tasha had somehow wrangled two toddlers into an impromptu sock-puppet drama called 'Kevin the Spoon's Final Reckoning.'

Sam just... stood.

Flapjack in one hand. Heart in the other.

Rupa joined her. Handed her a second flapjack, because some moments require reinforcement.

"We've become... contagious," she said.

"In a good way?"

"In a lentil-scented, glitter-adjacent, slightly unhinged way."

"I'll take that."

Ronnie, ever the barometer of begrudging approval, leaned over the counter.

"You lot are like glitter," they said. "Just when I think I've cleaned it all up, someone starts a biscuit empire or mends a pensioner's trousers with embroidered quotes."

Sam snorted. "We're sparkly chaos."

"Worse," muttered Ronnie. "You're useful."

Sam beamed.

Because no - she hadn't planned any of this.

She didn't build a brand.

She didn't write a manifesto.

She just... opened a door.

Started a group.

Made tea.

And people, somehow, filled the gaps.

They stitched each other together.

Shared skills like sweets.

Swapped stories with tea.

They weren't building resumes.

They were building lives.

Messy ones. Threadbare in places. But full of laughter and lint and the kind of meaning you don't notice until someone turns up with their own logo.

Later that day, Ash came back over and gave her a spare patch - **'Stitch Happens.'**

Sam tucked it into her coat pocket, already planning to sew it somewhere visible.

The Biscuit Legacy

Brenda, queen of budgeting, didn't mean to start another class.

She just brought biscuits.

That was it. No grand announcement. No laminated flyers or passive-aggressive group emails titled 'Let's Get Bready to Crumble.' Just biscuits. In a tin so battered it looked like it had survived at least two wars, a bingo riot, and a particularly heated debate about marzipan.

But oh, those biscuits.

They were so good, someone once described them as "life-changing, with a chewy core." Another person claimed they had a spiritual experience mid-shortbread and briefly saw the face of their late Aunt Doris in a custard cream swirl.

Even Ronnie - famously unmoved by anything except health and safety violations - paused after their first bite, narrowed their eyes at Brenda, and muttered, "You use butter. Real butter."

Brenda just shrugged. "I don't mess about."

One Thursday, the council paid a return visit, this time a smart young man turned up - clipboard, tie, the whole "I'm from the council and here to inspect your policies" vibe.

He was mid-sentence about infrastructure improvements and waste collection when Brenda handed him a ginger snap.

He blinked.

Paused.

Looked down at the biscuit like it had just proposed marriage.

"Do you cater?" he asked, voice soft with reverence.

Brenda snorted. "I cater to no one."

But it was too late. Word had spread.

Every time she entered the Workshop Café, there was a collective rustle of expectation. Like the Queen arriving at a bake sale. People perked up. Whispered. Took strategic positions near the biscuit tin.

"Is that..?"

"It is. The shortbread."

Someone asked how she made them.

Brenda, visibly horrified at the idea of giving away her secrets, muttered, "Bit of this, bit of that," and escaped to the teapot like it was a fire exit.

But the following week - and no one quite knows why - she turned up with a recipe.

Typed.

On paper.

With bullet points.

In Comic Sans.

We do not speak of the font.

The week after that, she brought flour.

Then rolling pins.

Then Doreen, chaos in an apron. The one who didn't know the difference between plain flour and self-raising.

And without quite meaning to... Brenda had a class.

She didn't announce it. She didn't name it. It was just, turn up, don't burn anything, and don't argue with Brenda about scones.

But eventually, the group gave it a name.

Rolling Pins & Rants.

The name stuck.

Much like the treacle tart to the bottom of someone's handbag.

It started with three regulars.

Then five.

Then ten.

Before long, Brenda was running the session like a slightly sweary Bake Off judge crossed with a particularly blunt therapist.

She offered praise with suspicious caution.

"That's not awful."

"I've seen worse."

"You've got potential. Don't let it go to your head."

"Soggy bottom - but nice flavour."

And scolded with devastating precision.

"You don't need a rolling pin, Doreen. You need a concrete bollard."

Her golden rule was: "Keep it honest. Keep it warm. And never trust anyone who says they don't like ginger nuts."

Brenda taught:

- How to make scones that didn't double as emergency construction material.

- The art of confident crimping.

- How to wield a rolling pin like you meant it, preferably while making a point about the decline of manners and the rise of margarine.

Someone - possibly Tasha - suggested she enter the town fair.

Brenda rolled her eyes so hard it caused a minor breeze.

"I'm not here for ribbons," she scoffed.

But she entered.

And won third prize.

For her shortbread.

She brought the rosette in the next day, casually tucked in her handbag between a bag of walnuts, a half-eaten croissant, and a shopping list that just said, "strong tea, justice."

"I suppose they were alright," she said, like it wasn't the baking equivalent of the Nobel Peace Prize.

Sam tried to hug her. Brenda tolerated it like someone being approached by a wet cat - stiff, confused, but not entirely resistant.

From that point on, the group crowned her with titles she absolutely did not ask for:

- 'The Crumb Commander.'

- 'Lady Shortbread of Biscuitshire.'

- 'The Flour Whisperer' (Tasha, obviously).

Brenda told them all to grow up. Then handed out another round of ginger snaps with the unspoken understanding that this was her version of a group hug.

One Thursday, while violently stirring a mixing bowl like it had personally wronged her, Brenda paused.

"Here's the thing," she said. "When I stopped baking, I stopped feeling useful."

Everyone went quiet.

Except Mo, who sneezed into a bag of caster sugar and apologised profusely to the spirit of baking.

Brenda stared into her bowl - flour on her nose, defiance in her shoulders, and something softer behind her eyes.

"You lot reminded me I've still got something worth sharing."

She held up a biscuit. "So, fine. You can have the recipe. But if anyone puts chocolate chips in it, I will haunt you."

Mo raised a hand, deadpan. "What if they're dark chocolate?"

"You'll get a mild haunting. Just cupboard rattling. Maybe a ghostly tut."

By the end of the month, 'Rolling Pins & Rants' was the most popular thing at the Workshop Café.

Even more than Tasha's 'Vegetables and You' sessions.

People brought their kids. Masha and her little girl turned up. Brenda even managed to find out her name,

Ira. Turns out she likes both chocolate chips and Brenda.

Someone brought their ex, and said, "If Brenda says we're both wrong, we are."

The café began to smell - permanently, beautifully - of cinnamon, butter, and second chances.

Sam stood at the back one afternoon, watching Brenda guide a teenager through the delicate process of creaming butter and sugar, and felt something shift inside her.

Pride.

But not the loud, Instagram-filtered kind.

The warm kind.

The kind that smells of vanilla and sticks to your ribs.

Later that day, as the last batch cooled and Brenda threatened to exile anyone who over-handled their dough, Sam whispered to Rupa, "She's not just baking."

Rupa smiled. "No. She's restoring."

Mo, nearby, nodded solemnly and muttered, "She's a biscuit-based miracle."

Ronnie passed by with a broom and said, "If she starts selling them, I want a cut."

They all laughed.

And Brenda - rolling her eyes, muttering about how silly everyone was getting over a few biscuits - passed round another tray.

From Numbers to New Starts

Pauline used to flinch at the word 'spreadsheet.'

Not metaphorically. Not gently. We're talking full-body recoil, as if someone had said, "team-building exercise" or "group karaoke."

The first time she came into the Workshop Café, she was following Brenda like a slightly nervous duckling. Clutching her handbag with both hands. Wide-eyed. Like someone had tricked her into walking into a maths-themed escape room.

She refused to even glance at the budgeting sheets.

"Nope," she said. "Numbers make me break out in sarcasm."

Brenda handed her a biscuit and grunted, "Same. But we push on."

That was week one.

By week seven?

Pauline turned up early.

With a folder.

An organised folder.

With tabs. And dividers. And - Sam swore this was true - a mini sticky note index shaped like penguins.

"Just in case someone needs a visual reference," Pauline had explained.

She now could be found helping in every one of Brenda's budgeting classes.

Gently. Kindly. With biscuits and coloured highlighters and the sort of calm you only achieve after surviving three utility bill meltdowns and finding the strength to call the helpline and hold for seventeen minutes.

She started with the basics.

What's a direct debit?

How do you know if it's essential?

Why do numbers hate us, and can we bribe them with snacks?

Lee had helped design the spreadsheet template. Crisp lines, logical layout, soothing colour palette. Budgeting, but make it fashion.

Pauline called him her "quiet calculator."

He pretended to be mildly offended.

"Could've gone with 'ninja of numerics,'" he muttered.

Then immediately fixed the biscuit cupboard drawer so he didn't have to say thank you.

But something had changed.

Pauline, who once panicked at the sight of a pound sign, now stood tall in the centre of the room, explaining fixed versus variable costs like a woman who'd stared into the financial abyss and come back with a laminated pie chart.

Then, one Thursday, she arrived… different.

Not dramatically. Just… subtle things.

A new blouse.

Shoes that said, "I'm here for an interview, but I still prioritise arch support."

A slight lift in her posture - like she was carrying herself rather than just her handbag.

Sam noticed it first.

"You okay?"

Pauline smiled, a little sheepishly. "I got a new job."

There was a beat of silence.

The kind of silence observed for spotting miracles or hearing that Brenda had willingly shared a recipe.

"A job?" Sam blinked. "Like… a real job?"

"Part-time. Charity office. Data entry. Nothing glamorous. But still."

Then chaos.

Brenda clapped her hands and shouted, "You clever cow!"

Tasha squealed, launched herself into a hug, and accidentally flung a budgeting pen halfway across the café.

Rupa gasped and immediately started baking something celebratory with apricot jam.

Pauline beamed. "They said I interviewed well. Said I seemed confident. Organised. Brought my own spreadsheet and everything."

Lee looked up sharply from his tea.

"You... brought a spreadsheet?"

She grinned. "Three, actually. Colour-coded. One with annotations."

Lee stared into his mug like it had betrayed him. Then started fixing the café door hinge with the intensity of a man processing feelings through carpentry.

Later, after the rush had faded and the biscuit crumbs had settled, Sam found him retightening screws that didn't need retightening.

"She did that because of you," she said gently.

He didn't look up. "She did that because of herself."

"You helped her see it was possible. You made numbers feel less scary."

"I just made a template."

"You gave her a map."

He paused. Then mumbled, "You cry too easily."

Sam smiled. "And you avoid compliments like they're unvaccinated toddlers."

He shrugged. "Just proud of her. That's all."

The next Saturday, Pauline came back.

She had a new handbag – slightly too large, suspiciously structured, definitely from a department store where the assistants call you *madam*.

She had a smile that lit up the corner of the café and made even Ronnie's new espresso machine hum approvingly.

And she had a gesture.

Not words. Not a speech. Just action.

She bought the first round of teas before anyone else could move, stacked them neatly on the table, then slid a packet of shortbread into the centre like an offering.

Sam paused mid-reach, realising what it meant. It was her way of saying: *thanks for believing in me*.

Lee noticed too. He didn't say anything.

But that afternoon, he left a new pen beside the sign-in sheet – one with four colours and a squishy grip.

The next week, 'Budget Buddies' was full, and there was no sign of Brenda.

Ronnie announced that her bus was delayed but Pauline was at the ready.

People came in clutching bills, mystery subscriptions, and slightly traumatised bank statements. Pauline welcomed them all with tea, calm, and a gentle threat involving highlighters and self-worth.

"You're allowed to not know," she told one man. "But now you've shown up, you're not allowed to stay confused. We'll figure it out."

By the end of the session, someone had made a savings plan.

Someone else had learned how to cancel three streaming services and breathe again.
And everyone left with a free biscuit and a folder tabbed like a rainbow.

That day, Sam watched from the doorway - Tasha tidying up laminated 'yes you CAN budget' posters, Mo organising chairs, Lee pretending not to smile - and felt it again.

That quiet ripple of pride.

That joy that bubbles under your ribs and makes your eyes go squishy.

Pauline, the woman who once said, "Excel sounds like a threat," now stood surrounded by people learning to see their finances as something they could hold - not fear.

The Workshop Café had taught a lot of things: how to sew buttons, bake scones, act like dramatic fruit, dodge council forms, and glitter-related bans.

But this?

This was real life.

Real skills.

Wrapped in tea and kindness and the kind of support you don't get from online tutorials with aggressive jazz intros.

And just like that, another chapter opened - in the margins of a spreadsheet, in the folds of a budget folder, between one woman's old fears and her brand-new confidence.

Rupa's Food, Everywhere

As revolutions go, this one simmered quietly in a slow cooker.

Rupa brought in the stew on a grim, rain-soaked Thursday in March. The sort of day that made pavements slippery, moods worse, and umbrellas question their will to live.

Rupa arrived just after 10:00 a.m., cardigan flapping like a flag of quiet defiance and a steaming pot tucked under one arm.

"It's not fancy," she said, placing it down on the café counter. "It's just... warm."

She said it like an apology.

But by the time the ladle reached the bottom of the pot, something had shifted.

Because it wasn't just warm.

It was... healing.

It was the edible equivalent of a hot water bottle and a reassuring hug. A beacon of hope. A mouthful of "you've got this."

By the end of lunch, three people had asked for the recipe, one person had cried mid-bite, and Tasha declared, "I think this just solved my childhood."

It was traditional English home cooking meets complex warming Indian spice.

Even Ronnie muttered something that might've been approval, though it was hard to tell - they were chewing and pretending not to care.

Rupa, flustered, scribbled the recipe on the back of an old bus receipt and passed it along.

"That's it," she said. "Nothing special. Just what was left in my fridge and a bit of guesswork."

That should've been the end of it.

But it wasn't.

Because a week later, someone photocopied the recipe.

Someone else added hand-drawn illustrations - including a smiley lentil with jazz hands.

Mo laminated a copy and tacked it to the kitchen wall beside the tea instructions.

Two weeks later, Rupa popped into the library to return a book and nearly dropped it when she spotted something on the noticeboard.

Her stew. In print. In the actual parish newsletter.

There it was in black and white:

Soup for the Soul – Community Recipes

Featuring: Leftover Lentil Miracle by 'Local Legend Rupa'

Rupa blinked.

Then backed slowly out of the library like she was being hunted by fame and laminated onions.

She stormed into the Workshop Café, cheeks pink with panic.

"It's not mine," she insisted.

Sam held up the original recipe. "Rupa. This is your handwriting. You literally drew a smiley next to 'add garlic.'"

Brenda leaned over, clutching her tea. "You're famous, love."

Rupa spluttered. "Don't be ridiculous."

"They're calling you 'The Lentil Queen.'"

Rupa dropped her spoon. "They what?!"

Mo nodded solemnly, as if delivering tragic news. "It's spreading. Like marmalade. But savoury."

And it really was.

Soon, people started turning up just to ask Rupa about batch cooking. About how to feed four people using one tin of tomatoes, three sad mushrooms, and the power of sheer determination.

They brought her onions. Bags of rice. Tupperware lids without bases - which she took with grace and a quiet sigh.

One woman, new to the group, said, "I didn't think I could cook. I thought cooking was for confident people who shop in Waitrose and own whisks that don't bend."

Rupa smiled. "If you've got a fork and low expectations, you can do more than you think."

And that was it.

Wednesday mornings became cooking club mornings.

Not that Rupa would call it that.

"There's no club," she insisted. "It's just people bringing leftovers and hoping for magic."

But magic kept showing up anyway.

They made:

- 'Korma-of-hope' (with whatever tins they could find and a brave amount of cumin - the kind Rupa's mum always said could rescue any bad day)

- 'Emergency crumble' (involving oats, pears, and a tragic but noble sacrifice of custard creams)

- 'Stuff-in-a-pan stew' (which turned out better than expected and now features on three fridge doors as a life-saving option)

There were no uniforms, no aprons - just a collection of humans armed with spoons, curiosity, and very flexible ideas about best-before dates.

Lee fixed the dodgy hob ring so it didn't sound like a dying goose every time it lit.
Mo made recipe cards with spaces to "add your own twist."

Tasha offered to write a theme song. Rupa politely declined.

Then one morning, Sam burst in, holding a flyer aloft like it was the scroll of destiny.

It read:

Rupa's Kitchen Club
Community Cooking at The Workshop Café
Recipes. Rescues. Remarkably Good Soup.

Wednesdays, 10 a.m.

(Lentils likely. Kindness guaranteed.)

Rupa stared at it.

Sam grinned. "So... we're official?"

Rupa groaned. "I liked it better when it was casual chaos."

Brenda patted her on the back. "Chaos is still there, love. It's just better fed now."

Ronnie glanced over. "If we're charging rent to vegetables, I want royalties."

Later that day, Rupa quietly began printing recipe cards on the café printer.

She laminated them herself.

And although she still rolled her eyes every time someone called her "The Lentil Queen," Sam caught her once - just once - smiling at the title and straightening the corner of the flyer like it mattered.

Because the truth was... she loved it.

Not the fame.

Not the name.

But the fact that something she cooked - something warm, simple, honest - had travelled.

Had made someone feel less alone.

Had taken root in cupboards and conversations and casserole dishes.

The Workshop Café now smelled like nutmeg, garlic, and purpose.

And every time someone walked in carrying a Tupperware of mystery veg and hope, Rupa would nod, tie on her (reluctantly adorable) apron, and say, "Right then. Let's turn this into something."

And they always did.

Because when Rupa cooked?

People listened.

Hearts softened.

And miracles - pale, steaming, and oddly lentil-based - happened quietly in bowls across the room.

Ronnie Gets Emotional (Sort Of)

It began with chalk dust and silence. Which, at The Workshop Café, usually meant someone was about to have a feeling - and Ronnie wouldn't like it.

Sam stood at the blackboard, carefully wiping away the faded words of last week's schedule. The chalk squeaked like it was auditioning for a horror film. Ronnie, passing with a tray of mugs, flinched so hard they nearly weaponised a teaspoon.

"You should buy a whiteboard or one of those flashy screens you can write on," they muttered.

"But then we'd lose the charm," Sam replied, drawing a wobbly star next to "Fix Your Trousers Friday" and a suspiciously abstract banana near "Drama with Tasha."

Ronnie huffed the way only someone emotionally allergic to whimsy can. They didn't stop walking. Just paused - slightly - to stare at the board.

Then, in the kind of voice you'd expect from someone confessing to liking decaf tea, they said,

"You lot... you've done something decent here."

Sam blinked.

"Wait. Was that... a compliment?"

Ronnie's face twitched. "No. It was a noise. Could've been indigestion."

"You said 'decent.' That's basically glowing praise coming from you."

"Don't push it," they snapped, already halfway to the kitchen, muttering darkly about soap dispensers and emotional manipulation.

Sam didn't push it.

She grinned instead. Like someone who'd just been told the family cat tolerated their presence.

But the next morning?

Sam found the card.

Taped beneath the counter, just below the till, beside a spoon that had been wedged there since April.

It was plain. No glitter. No name.

Just an envelope.

Inside:

To the gang in the back room –
You brought people together.

You made space where there wasn't any.

You did good.

Now stop making me say nice things.

Seriously. Stop it.

~ R

Sam stared at it.

Then read it again.

Then once more for good luck.

She smiled so hard she nearly sprained her face.

She marched into the café, holding the card like a trophy.

"Who left this?" she asked, voice echoing off teapots and tired floorboards.

Ronnie, polishing spoons with the intensity of someone removing all emotion via cutlery, didn't look up.

"No idea," they said. "Probably that Brenda woman. She's always scribbling things."

"But it's signed 'R.'"

"Could be Rita. Or Roberta. Or... Rage-fuelled Rachel. Heard she's quite sentimental."

Mo wandered over, took one look, and whispered, "They're proud of us."

"They're pretending not to be proud of us," Sam whispered back.

"Same thing," said Lee, walking past with a screwdriver and a mysterious piece of wood he may or may not have stolen from a bench.

From that day, small things started changing.

No announcements. No declarations. Just... quiet shifts.

Ronnie started making "extra" tea. Not for themself, obviously. Just in case. Just in case someone new wandered in, looked lost, or mentioned a difficult Tuesday.

They labelled the biscuit tins. With actual labels. Not just "mystery" and "do not eat unless insured."

They laminated Rupa's soup rota.

They replaced the spoon stuck under the counter.

And then - and this shook the group to its mismatched core - they let them hang bunting.

Just one strand.

In the corner.

But it stayed up. And every now and then, Sam caught them looking at it.

Like it might start singing.

Or worse - spark joy.

One Tuesday afternoon, Sam spotted Ronnie standing at the door watching.

Two people were learning to knit. One was showing off a painted flower pot. A toddler was dancing with a spoon and a deep sense of purpose.

"You built the bones," Sam said gently, sliding over with two mugs of tea.

Ronnie didn't look away.

"I just didn't stop you."

"That's half the battle," Sam said.

Ronnie passed her a tea towel.

"Go mop something. You're making me feel things."

Sam took the towel with a grin. "Admit it. You like us."

"I tolerate you."

"That's affection in Ronnie-speak."

"Careful," Ronnie muttered. "I might revoke biscuit privileges."

Sam laughed.

But she knew.

Underneath the sarcasm and steel-toe boots, Ronnie cared.

They always had.

They were the grumpy heartbeat of the place. The unofficial bouncer of feelings.

The silent approver of second chances. The guardian of mugs and moments.

The Flat

He was always just… there.

Not in the sock-puppet, jazz-hand way Tasha preferred. Not in the sweeping, biscuit-decreeing manner of Brenda. And certainly not in Sam's colour-coded, caffeine-fuelled blur.

Dave was quieter than all that.

Every Wednesday, he arrived just before budgeting started. Always on time. Never a fuss.

He didn't flinch when Pauline got passionate about interest rates. He didn't sigh when the soup was beige again. He just… helped. Stacked chairs. Rolled up tea towels. Unblocked the back loo that one time and said nothing about it.

If anyone had tried to describe him, they might've said, "You know… Dave?" and hoped that was enough.

And honestly, it often was.

Because in a space stitched together by noise and nerves and novelty jumpers, Dave's steady presence was its own kind of comfort. Like a dependable mug. Or that one good pen that never leaks.

He didn't speak much. But he stayed.

And in places like The Workshop Café, staying means something.

Then came 'That Wednesday'.

Tasha was running a very intense debate in the corner about whether Jaffa Cakes were biscuits or cakes ("It's a tax issue, not a snack!"), and someone had just spilled lentils into the sugar jar.

Business as usual.

And then, Dave cleared his throat.

Not dramatically. Not in a "cue the dramatic background music" kind of way.

Just a small sound, like he was testing whether the air would let him speak.

Sam looked up from the sign-in sheet. "Everything alright?"

He nodded. Then said, with all the ceremony of a weather report, "I got a flat."

That was it.

Simple.

Unassuming.

Like he'd just found a tenner in his coat pocket.

Sam blinked. "You mean... a place to live?"

He nodded again. "Signed the papers yesterday. My own place."

And for a heartbeat, the whole café stilled.

Even the kettle paused, as if it wanted to hear that again.

Then came the explosion.

Tasha gasped so loud it startled a nearby biscuit.

"You absolute legend!"

Brenda slammed her mug down. "About bloody time!"

Mo beamed so widely he actually spilled tea - which, for Mo, is akin to fireworks.

Lee let out a noise that could've been a cheer or a deeply repressed sob. Hard to tell with Lee.

And Sam just stood there.

Heart full. Eyes wide.

Watching Dave reach into his coat pocket and pull out a key.

He held it up.

Shiny. Ordinary. Life-changing.

"I've never had one before," he said, voice soft. "Not just mine. Not with my name on the letterbox."

Tasha promptly burst into tears and launched herself at him. The hug was so enthusiastic his glasses did a small somersault and landed in a nearby custard cream.

"Careful," Dave chuckled. "I've only just started breathing properly again."

They threw him an impromptu party. Obviously.

Someone found a slightly stale cake. Brenda declared it "perfectly celebratory if you eat around the edges."

Tasha presented a tea towel she'd attacked with permanent marker that read: KEY MASTER (beneath which she'd drawn what might have been a flat... or a lopsided sandwich).

Sam pulled Dave aside near the counter and handed him a brand-new mug.

White, with bold lettering on the front:

The Workshop Café.

So, you don't forget us.

He ran his thumb over the words like they were etched in gold.

"I didn't think this was possible," he said. "Not for me."

Sam smiled. "It is. Was. Is. You did this."

He looked at her, something flickering behind his glasses. "You all helped."

She shrugged. "We just made tea. You made the leap."

He nodded. "Yeah. I suppose I did."

The next Wednesday, he came back.

Of course he did.

With photos.

One of his blue front door.

One of a small plant on the windowsill ("Might be basil. Might be a weed. Either way, I'm feeding it.")

And one of a rug. Bright. Clashing. Clearly chosen with hope rather than coordination.

He said he'd started learning to cook. Said he liked it quiet. Said it still felt strange to shut the door behind him and know - deep in his bones - that it was his.

"It's mine," he whispered again, more to himself than anyone.

Mo immediately offered to build him a key hook. "To stop it getting lost."

Rupa handed over a recipe for "first-night noodles," which mostly involved garlic, comfort, and something resembling sauce.

Brenda looked him up and down and declared, "Right. From now on, you're Lord Flattington."

Even Ronnie smiled. A real one. The kind that lasted more than three seconds and might've briefly lit up the plug socket behind them.

They framed a copy of his door photo.

Stuck it on the wall beside the blackboard.

Right under "Soup-as-Therapy" and just above "Sew & Swear (adults only)."

No label. No plaque.

Just a key.

But everyone knew what it meant.

That it was possible.

That all the little things - the biscuits, the budgeting sessions, the quiet nods and folded chairs and shared soup - added up.

To safety.

To belonging.

To a front door you could lock at night and call your own.

Dave still comes every Wednesday.

Still helps stack chairs.

Still doesn't say much.

But every now and then, someone glances at the photo on the wall and smiles.

Sam's Doubts

Halfway through the second bite of toast, it crept in.

Not a grand realisation - more like background static slowly turning up the volume. That strange, restless feeling that makes you pause mid-butter, staring into the marmalade like it's got life advice and a backup plan.

The drop-in was buzzing.

There was laughter from the sewing corner, where Mo was supervising a button-based emergency with the same gravitas most people reserved for open-heart surgery.

The smell of lentils floated through the room, daring someone to make a bad soup joke and be disowned by Rupa.

Over by the window, Tasha had wrangled a handful of sugar-fuelled children into what she claimed was a re-enactment of last night's thunderstorm.

In the corner, an old man Sam didn't recognise was teaching a student how to rewire their broken desk lamp.

It was brilliant.

It was beautiful.

And it was running without her.

Sam stood by the tea urn, her toast cooling in her hand, and wondered - not for the first time in recent weeks - if she was still... needed.

Brenda had become a baking oracle, casually ending mild existential panic with perfectly timed ginger nuts.

Rupa was on recipe rota number four, ending food poverty one chickpea at a time and somehow managing to make community cooking feel like a Michelin event in a village hall.

Tasha had transformed every corner of the room into a stage. There were scarf-based soliloquies. Interpretive plant pot monologues. Kids who now requested "emotional warm-ups" before lunch.

Lee had installed another coat rack, reinforced the tea shelf, and - without fanfare - mounted a small wooden ledge above the biscuit tin labelled:

Emotional Tools

Sam didn't know whether to laugh or cry, so she just stared at her clipboard instead.

It was, at this point, mostly doodles. And a half-eaten ginger snap.

She used to colour-code schedules. Now she was inventing new species of biscuit monsters in biro.

She didn't sew. She couldn't bake without setting off smoke alarms. She once attempted a minor fix on a chair and ended up with a bruise shaped like France.

She just... started it.

That's all.

And now?

Now it was growing. Moving. Breathing. Without her constant input.

Which, according to every book on leadership she'd ever panic-borrowed from the library, was a sign of success.

But it didn't feel like success.

It felt like being the kid who organised the party, put up the balloons, and then stood in the corner watching everyone else dance.

She wiped down a table that didn't need wiping. Rearranged the menus. Wondered, for the first time, if it might be time to step back. Quietly. Gently.

She could just drift to the edges. Let the kettle boil for someone else. Maybe take up silent yoga. Or train as a librarian.

Mo spotted her from across the room.

Of course he did.

Mo noticed everything - shifts in atmosphere, threads that came loose, people who smiled with their mouths but not their eyes.

Five minutes later, he was beside her.

Silent as always.

Holding a mug.

The tea was exactly the right temperature.

Of course it was. He was Mo.

He passed it to her without a word.

She took it. Sipped. Perfect.

"You alright?" he asked.

Sam attempted a shrug. "Just... wondering if I'm still useful."

Mo blinked once. Tilted his head. Then said, "You are the kettle."

She blinked back. "I... what?"

"You're the kettle," he repeated. "You got everything boiling. Now we're just keeping the temperature going."

She laughed - a short, surprised snort. "That's ridiculous."

"Is it?" he asked.

She looked around.

At Pauline in the corner, calmly explaining highlighter strategy to someone terrified of bills.

At Brenda passing around what she called her "Mood Muffins" (no one dared ask what that meant).

244

At Ash - hoodie mogul and reluctant youth mentor - helping a teenager with stubborn pride and fluorescent thread.

At the noticeboard, now a layered collage of sessions, events, ideas. Most of which Sam hadn't organised. Many of which she didn't even recognise. But all of them born from the thing she started.

All of them running.

Breathing.

Living.

Without her clipboard.

She let out a slow breath. "I guess I boiled."

Mo nodded. "You still do. Quietly. In the background. But we know."

She bumped her shoulder against his. "You're annoyingly good at this, you know?"

He sipped his tea. "I just stitched it together. Nothing fancy."

They stood there for a while.

Two friends.

Two mugs.

One warm silence.

Watching what they'd built - not through force, or structure, or spreadsheets - but through kindness. And showing up. And saying 'yes' even when they didn't know how.

Sam took another sip.

She didn't need to run everything.

She didn't need to be the best at anything.

She was the kettle.

She got things boiling.

One Year Later

It was supposed to be low-key.

Just a casual, "Oh look, it's been a year, let's eat cake and maybe not cry" kind of thing. A quiet nod. A cup of tea. Possibly a card. Maybe someone would bring Jaffa Cakes if things got wild.

But this was the Workshop Café.

Low-key had long since packed up, left the building, and been replaced by bunting and chaos.

You can't quietly celebrate twelve months of laughter, lentils, and life-altering group hugs with plain digestives and a polite nod.

So naturally, there were:

- Fairy lights (despite Ronnie's official protest and unofficial approval),

- Bunting (smuggled in after closing time like rebellious confetti),

- And a massive handmade banner that read:

HAPPY BIRTHDAY ALL OF US

Before the doors even opened, people were lining up outside.

Some brought baked goods.

Some brought hugs.

Some brought nervous smiles and the words, *"I used to come here, and... I thought I'd just pop in."*

They weren't just visitors. They were pieces of the story.

Ash, the teenager with the custom hoodies brought stitched tea towels that read:

Stirred, Not Shaken.

Pauline turned up flashing her work lanyard like it was an Olympic medal. She wore it all afternoon, even while lugging trestle tables.

Rupa arrived with five cakes. Brenda judged four of them. Fiercely. The fifth one was hers.

Ash set up a photo wall, before-and-after shots, not just of projects, but of people. A jacket repaired. A frown turned grin. A cardboard crown worn with pride.

And then there was Masha, with her shy little daughter Ira. Ira had a notebook clutched tight to her chest, pages stuffed with pencil sketches. She hesitated for ages before showing it to Brenda.

Inside? Portraits of everyone.

Sam mid-glue disaster. Tasha with jazz hands bigger than her head. Ronnie scowling affectionately over a kettle. Even Brenda herself, drawn with a biscuit crown.

Brenda blinked. Then beamed.

Within minutes she was parading Ira's notebook around the room like a priceless treasure. The pictures were pinned up along the bunting, each one greeted with cheers, laughter, and the occasional embarrassed blush.

By the time Ira ducked behind her mum's legs again, she had an entire café of people telling her she was brilliant.

"We should frame these," said Mo.

And then Ronnie arrived.

Late. Of course.

Holding the cake.

It was square-ish. Possibly lemon. Iced in what could best be described as enthusiastic swirls and dangerous peaks. Slightly leaning, like it had contemplated quitting halfway through baking.

They slammed it onto the table.

"I baked," Ronnie declared. "It's a moment. Don't make it weird."

Rupa went hunting for a knife. Couldn't find one. So, Lee picked up a screwdriver and ceremonially cut the cake like he was rewiring a toaster.

"Symbolic," Sam announced. "I love it."

Someone called for a speech.

Tasha stood on a chair, blinked back tears, made it three lines into a heartfelt thank-you, then accidentally quoted Shakespeare and collapsed into a curtain.

Mo raised a biscuit. "Cheers."

And somehow, that was enough.

They all joined in — mugs of tea of every shape and size, chipped enamel cups, even one lovingly washed bowl raised high.

"To the things we didn't plan."

"To the place we built anyway."

"To the skills we swapped, and the selves we found."

"To one year."

"To the next."

And then, lovely quiet Dave, who always showed up but never stood out, said "To creating family" and with a cheeky wink pulled out an enormous party popper and pulled the string.

Glitter, confetti and sparkles rained down over the gang and they all laughed with joy – even Ronnie.

Could You Spare a Moment?

Well... you made it. Through the biscuit carnage, the dodgy power poses, and the needle that nearly took me out. Gold star for you.

If this story made you laugh, cry, or just nod in messy recognition, a quick Amazon review would mean the world. Nothing fancy - even *"Yes, there were biscuits"* will do.

Thanks for reading. Thanks for being here. Now go put the kettle on – and maybe grab a biscuit.

Printed in Dunstable, United Kingdom